THE HELIX HERBAL ALBUM

THE HELIX HERBAL ALBUM

by
Rick Roen and
R. Kim Finley

Illustrated by Sandra Dutton

Recipes and
Technical Information
by Arnold L. Manheimer

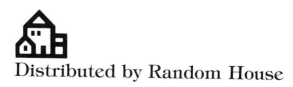

Distributed by Random House

RFM Publishing Corporation
Boulder, Colorado 80306

ACKNOWLEDGEMENTS:
For collaboration on the research and writing
of this book we'd like to thank *Jean Strueber*
whose tireless support helped complete the
project, *Steve Kornher* for gathering the
information on companion and lunar planting,
Les Steinau for his personal interest,
encouragement and advice, and
Annette L. Thompson whose last minute editing
put the contents of this book within the grasp
of the world's English-speaking people.

SPECIAL THANKS to the staff at
Random House for their help, patience
and encouragement in developing this book.

Published in the United States by
RFM Publishing Corporation, Boulder, Colorado
and Distributed in the United States
by Random House, Inc.

Printed in the United States of America
by Eastwood Printing, Denver, Colorado

23456789

73654-0

Contents:

Introduction

The exact date when modern man's collective mental eye began to look again at herbs has been obscured. But it would be safe to say that the word "herb" entered the broad spectrum of vernacular speech sometime during the Granola Age of the late sixties and early seventies.

Old herbals and information on herbs began to be resurrected from the dusty corners of libraries, the back shelves of bookstores, and from behind the paregoric of small-town pharmacies. When it was found, the volume of information was minutely detailed, often needed translating, and in short was overwhelming.

For the serious herb gardener, this presented a challenge. But for the gardener with a casual interest in growing herbs, it presented a problem. After all, you shouldn't have to go back for a master's degree just to have fun in the garden. A successful first planting should be the place to start. And that's where we come in.

The purpose of this book is to introduce you to a useful assortment of garden-variety herbs in a way that is easy, economical, and painless; to guide you through your first planting; to stand by when your first green shoots sprout up; and to humbly step aside after a successful harvest.

The packets of herb seeds included with this book are only the beginning. In the following pages, you'll find general information and ideas on laying out an herb garden with hints on sun, soil, and watering. Included are ways to preserve what you've grown, recipes, and uses. Herbs are featured alphabetically, each in its own special section. This is a more individual account of planting, growing and use with details on herb history and folklore.

Some of this information may seem to overlap or be repetitious. This is done simply to build your confidence, give you the freedom to fearlessly persevere, and put to rest, once and for all, your herbal anxieties.

We've chosen the herbs described in this book for a particular reason. In putting together a collection of herbs, we feel it's only right to provide you with a respectable variety that cross-sections Herbdom.

The herb seeds we've selected to accompany this book respond to a variety of conditions, growing both indoors and out, and are commonly found in the United States. Growing performance has been considered above all. Through experience we know that nothing dampens the excitement of growing something more than seeing your leaf come up limp and anemic. Following the directions in this book, the hardest part of growing your herb garden should be the sleepless nights spent waiting for the first little plants to sprout.

Problems may come up. At the end of this book we've listed a number of publications any one of which can provide answers to your questions. You should be able to find them in your local library, garden center, or health-food store. If any of your plants fail to germinate after following the instructions let us know. Send us a letter with all of the gory details and include a stamped, self-addressed envelope. We'll mail you more seeds and you can try again.

There may be other herbs mentioned in this book that you wish to grow. Send us your request by using the order form at back of the book. For your convenience, we've listed the complete line of herb seeds available from Helix.

And now, let's go dig in the dirt!

A Word Before We Begin...

lthough we've kept botanical terminology to a minimum for your reading ease, there are a few terms used throughout this book that may not be familiar. Here's a quick study in some of the plant terms that should be familiar to every herb gardener.

Herbs, like other plants, can be divided into three categories based on the length of their life cycle. *Annuals* last only one season, coming up from seed, completing growth, flowering, and going to seed within the same year. They must be replanted each year, unless the plant is allowed to reseed itself for the next year's crop. *Biennials* complete their growth cycle across two years, producing flowers and going to seed during the second year. *Perennials* are long-lasting plants that come up year after year from the same roots. They are often planted in a permanent location where they should not be disturbed.

Temperature, too, affects the life cycle of plants. Herbs referred to as *hardy* can survive cold winters well (in the case of perennials and biennials) and do not require continuously warm temperatures before planting outdoors when starting. Hardy annuals, for example, would never survive a winter because of their life cycle, but can generally be started from seed outdoors in the early spring. Hardy perennials, once started, should grow well in the north, and may, in some cases, actually grow better under cool conditions. *Tender* plants, on the other hand, can't take the cold, regardless of how long they would live normally. Some tender perennials may survive the winters in the north but only if protected and well mulched; others must be brought indoors for the coldest months.

1

Starting,& Growing& theTransition Outdoors

Grown indoors, herbs are a welcome addition to the home year-round. During the winter months, savory, thyme, tarragon, marjoram, and basil not only brighten the dark days but freshen the home with their scents. In the summer, a hanging basket of thyme or a small pot of chives on the kitchen window sill, as a source of fresh herbs is convenient and can be easily clipped to garnish or flavor cold drinks and light summer salads.

When you start planning where to grow your herbs, give careful consideration to how they will be grown.

It's possible to start many herbs indoors and move them outside; some grow outside (normally because of their size) or inside entirely; while others are started inside, moved outside, and then brought back in during the winter.

Check the instructions for growing each before you make a decision on where to start and how you grow your herbs. Parsley, for example, does not transplant well. You're apt to want it continually, so consider growing it in a pot indoors, or in a pot that can be moved outdoors when the weather is warm.

Catnip is another exception: The plant itself doesn't mind transplanting, but the transplanting process will stir up enough catnip scent to attract every cat in the neighborhood. You will want to grow it outside, and it's best to start it there.

Starting Herbs Indoors

To begin indoors, first consider where you will grow your herbs. The location you choose must be close at hand, where your herbs can get four or five hours of direct sun each day. Since plants tend to grow toward the sun, a quarter-turn each week is recommended to keep them full. They must also be kept moist at first to encourage development, so you'll need to locate your plants where it's easy to water them. Finally, you'll need to locate your plants where there is good ventilation but where there are no strong drafts.

Once you have found a place where these needs can be met, you are ready to get materials. In addition to seeds, you'll need some small peat pots or flats. Both can be purchased at your local garden-supply center. Better yet, you can also use cardboard milk containers, cut in half lengthwise, instead of purchased flats. Small holes should be punched in the bottom of these for drainage. As a growing medium, any standard potting soil will do for planting. If you want to mix your own, a formula familiar to most gardeners is the blending of equal parts of garden loam, peat moss, and sand.

Herb seeds should be planted to the depth indicated for the individual herb. Most seed packets give this information, but it's also available in this book under the care and cultivation section for each herb. A good rule of thumb is to plant to a depth of three times the seed diameter. If you're left with any doubt, it's better to err by planting deeper; shallow-rooted plants have a tendency to tip over. Check the instructions, too, on whether the seeds should be covered with soil. Some herb seeds need light to germinate.

Herbs like a warm, moist environment for germination, and a temperature of 70–75°F during the day; 65–68°F at night will work well for most. The moisture, and to some extent the warmth, can be controlled by placing a loose-fitting plastic bag over the pots or flats. Punching a few holes in the bag will allow for some ventilation, but do not assume this is enough. The bag must be removed for a few hours each day so the soil doesn't mold.

If your plants dry out, you either are leaving the bag

off too long or aren't watering enough.

Watering is best done by putting the pots or flats in a tray of water to stand for 30 to 45 minutes. When you use this method, the soil will absorb adequate moisture and you won't run the risk of damaging the young plants with an errant stream of water.

When you water, a word of caution: Many major cities heavily fluoridate and chlorinate their water supplies, which can be detrimental to young plants. These chemicals can be evaporated simply by letting the water stand overnight in an open container. This also allows the water to warm or cool to room temperature, which decreases any shock to the plant.

On the average, perennial herbs are slow to start, so be patient with them. Annuals and biennials should pop up within a week to ten days, grow quickly for a few days, and then slow down while developing a root system.

Plant failure usually is the result of not properly balancing heat and moisture, but overwatering can be just as bad. Watch your seedlings closely and adjust heat and moisture as necessary.

Transplanting to the Outdoors

When your young herbs are growing well and the second set of leaves has appeared, it's time to transplant, providing the weather is warm. May is generally a good month to make the move, though earlier transplanting is possible if the danger of frost is past.

The transition to the outdoors should begin with the process known as hardening off. This allows the plants to adapt slowly to the new environment.

You can begin hardening off your herbs by putting your pots or flats outdoors during the day. Place in the shade for a few hours, and bring back inside. Over a week, gradually increase the amount of light and length of time outside. After seven days the plants should become adjusted. How do you tell? Plant growth is the indicator. The young leaves will change color slightly and take on a more hardy, outdoor appearance.

Now is the time.

If you've used peat pots, the transition is simple. Dig a hole and put in the plant, pot and all. The peat containers are easiest to transplant, and they enrich the soil around the growing herbs as they break down.

If you've used flats, you're going to have to dig up each plant individually. Use a spoon to dig it up, taking with it a ball of soil around the roots. The spoon also can be used to steady the plant as you put it in the ground. If you must handle the plant, either cup the ball of soil in your hand or hold a bottom leaf and spare the fragile stem. Gently adjust the plant so that it stands straight, and press firmly into place. Watering immediately will help to settle it into its new home.

4

Transplanting a tender seedling is a time to be gentle. If you think about what the trauma must be like for a young plant, you will understand. The plant is going from a place where it is warm, humid, and just right, to a harsh outdoors, where it is colder at night and often hotter during the day. There are bugs and bacteria to both help and harm the plant, green crawly things for its leaves, and brown snaky things to squirm around its roots. The more understanding and care you apply at this point, the better your plants will do.

Once the initial trauma has passed, the young plants should adapt well to their new environment, provided they are watched carefully and watered with a gentle hand.

Starting Herbs Outdoors

In general, only the very hardy herbs should be started outdoors; more tender plants should be started indoors and transplanted. Those herbs that you intend to grow outdoors or that don't transplant well should be started outside. Usually, growing instructions are specific when planting time is mentioned. Take note, some herbs may be started early in the growing season; others require that there be no danger of frost.

Sow the seeds at the time indicated for each herb, paying attention to the soil conditions required for its growth. If you've judged the season properly, the temperature should be about right, but you also have to watch the amount of sun to ensure the seedlings will get enough, but not too much. Again, check the individual instructions. Water gently. You can soak the ground around the herbs without directly watering them, or you can use a gentle spray to soak the area.

Growing Herbs Indoors

Herbs can be grown indoors as pot herbs simply by starting them in permanent pots that you plan to keep inside. For all, natural light is best but some of them grow equally well under fluorescent lights. Regardless, green herbs make the house look great, smell good, and allow you to have herbs for use in their best state—fresh.

If you wish to grow a large number of herbs in the house, consider a window box instead of pots. Or use both so you can have a small indoor garden in one spot and bright sprigs of color in other places.

The only difficulty you may encounter with pot herbs is in transplanting. Start your plants as instructed above, and as each plant grows, move it to a larger pot. Place stones or flower-pot chards over the drainage hole and put in potting soil. Transplanting methods like those previously mentioned can be used. Frequently, you can simply loosen the entire contents of the old pot and move it to a new pot, adding soil around the edges and underneath.

Growing Outside

As your herbs grow from tender seedlings to mature plants, the greatest change you will have to make is in watering. Gradually adopt the watering schedule needed by the mature plant, noting the relative dryness of the soil. Some herbs need the same moist environment throughout their growth cycles; others need less water as they mature. Outdoor temperature and the amount of sun will affect the soil moisture, and you should replenish the moisture when needed. Aside from water, herbs need very little regular care. Simple pinching back (pruning) will suffice to produce a bushy growth that will provide you with plenty of herb leaves to harvest.

Transplanting from Outdoors to the Inside

If you have planted tender perennials, you may want to bring them inside during the winter months to assure growth the next year. Even hardy perennials may be brought in, simply because you want to keep them growing through the winter months to enjoy their fresh leaves.

Transplanting from outdoors is easiest when you plan ahead. Herbs that you will want to bring in can be planted in pots. These can be taken outside in the spring and then brought back in at the end of summer. The pots often are sunk into the earth of the herb garden during the summer to simplify care.

If you haven't preplanted in pots, the process is still fairly easy. Dig the plant out of the ground, complete with plenty of soil, put it in a pot, and bring it inside. Although minor root damage is easily overcome, care should be taken so that the roots are not too severely harmed. Moved correctly, your plants then should do well inside.

Harvest & Drying

If you're new to the world of fresh herbs—with the exception of perhaps parsley or a few chives from your neighbor's garden—you probably think of herbs primarily as dried seasonings. True, when properly dried and stored, herbs will retain many of their fresh characteristics, and this quality is what makes them so beloved of cooks. But when used daily during the growing season, in cooking, for making summer drinks, or as a garnish, freshly harvested herbs are herbs at their peak —when they are most fragrant, most tasty, most colorful and elegant.

Reaping the Benefits

When you think about harvesting your herbs, give some thought to gathering both herbs to use fresh during the summer and herbs to be dried for the winter. It's easy to assume that what you harvest for summer use is going to deplete that to be harvested for winter use, but this is not true. Continual pinching back throughout the growing season actually benefits many herb plants. They, in turn, respond with a more spirited, bushier growth, which produces a healthier, more prolific harvest. Most herbs grow so rapidly that you can harvest as many as three crops for drying during the summer, as well as what is taken for immediate use. So enjoy your herbs both in the summer and the winter.

7

If you've grown herbs indoors, your supply can be continuous. Perennials will continue to yield, and annuals can be planted at such times that you have access to them year round. When grown outdoors, however, the supply of fresh herbs is temporal at best, and many may be sadly depleted by an unpredicted frost or crop failure. Certainly, the supply from outdoor annuals ends with the coming of winter. By proper harvesting and drying, herbs can yield fresh-tasting seasonings that last for several years. Here is where herbs display their most valuable characteristic.

To harvest for drying, you cut off a major section of the plant, rather than small bunches of leaves. In most cases, the time to harvest is just prior to flowering. There's a reason for this. In order to produce flowers, the plant redirects energy previously put into growing leaves. Though the leaves appear not to change, their flavor and potency are diminished, and you harvest to get the best your plant has to offer. Harvest what you need, leaving enough growth for the plant to bush out again, unless you are harvesting an annual at the end of the season, in which case you take the whole plant. When harvesting the flowers of the plant, as you would in the case of borage and lavender, or if you want the seeds, as you would with dill, fennel or coriander, harvest occurs after the plant flowers, and you wait until later in the plant's cycle.

It is helpful, when you have finished cutting back an herb plant, to bundle together all the cuttings from that particular variety and label them. If you are going to grow a number of herbs and harvest them several times each, you're going to be drying a lot of herbs, and it will be easy to confuse one with another. Labeling eliminates any chance of this.

Preserving What You've Grown

When drying and storing herbs, you try to preserve as much of the taste and aroma of the fresh herb as possible. Understanding why herbs taste and smell as they do will help you to better understand the drying process. Within the herb leaves, seeds and flowers, minute glands encapsulate essential oils of the plant. It is these essential oils that flavor and scent the herb. A delicate balance exists within the plant between the holding and releasing of these oils. Crushing or infusing will, of course, break open these oil cells, but slight bruising and even small amounts of heat will do the same, in many cases.

The main objective in drying is to preserve these essential oils within the plant. In so doing, the same herbal flavors and aromas known to the ancients and the medieval herbalists can become available to you whenever you desire.

The first step in drying is to handle your plants gently to

8

avoid bruising and the second is to cure them properly. A latter section of this chapter will spell out general drying instructions. Before we generalize, though, let's concentrate on the specifics of curing your plants. Three major factors must be controlled when drying herbs and these are:

Heat

One can easily see the effect of heat on herbs by noticing that an herb patch is much more fragrant on a hot, sunny day than on a cool, cloudy one. The intense heat from the sun causes rapid evaporation of the oils, filling the air with their herbal vapors. In drying, the same is true: The oils, a desired element in cooking, potpourris and teas, will vaporize and dissipate in too much heat. On the other hand, too little heat can be just as bad. Not enough heat may cause the herbs to dry too slowly, allowing them to retain moisture, resulting in mold covering your carefully grown and harvested plants.

What, then, is the correct amount?

Generally, a warm attic or a dry room 75–100°F works well for most herbs. In this situation they can remain for some time, drying slowly. Some, however, need to be dried faster than these conditions permit. Basil, for instance, will turn brown quickly and lose its flavor if not dried within two or three days after picking. Here, an oven works best. Set the temperature on low about 150°F, spread the leaves out, and turn them frequently so they can dry evenly. A few hours at this temperature should suffice. Remember: the heat used in cooking should release the herbs' flavor, not the heat used in drying.

Light

Avoid it! With few exceptions, direct sunlight will discolor your herbs, will evaporate the essential oils, and will result in less attractive, less palatable seasonings. This is true both when drying your herbs and when storing them after drying. We don't mean to imply that you should hang black drapes in your drying room and check the drying process only by candlelight, but, in general, the less light the better.

Moisture

This is what you are trying to take out of your plants. In dry climates, such as most of the Western United States, there is little problem with moisture, but in the more humid climates, moisture can slow the drying process so much that the herbs become stale and moldy.

Air circulation is a must.

Any well-vented room can serve as a drying room. It's also helpful to bundle the plants loosely so that air can circulate between the leaves and a fan in the drying room will often greatly speed up the process. As a last resort, don't forget the oven—other herbs can be dried just like the basil described above.

Storing

Storing herbs requires the same considerations of heat, light, and moisture. Herbs should be kept in containers that will not allow the essential oils to escape. Glass jars are highly recommended. Plastic containers are just "OK." Plastic and paper bags rate low because they're either semi-porous or porous allowing herb flavors to dissipate on contact with the air. Whichever container you select, storage in a cupboard will protect your herbs from light; this, in turn, guarantees their flavor and color much longer. When storing your herbs, the tendency is to place them near the stove for convenience. Don't. Keeping them in any warm place is not desirable. Finally, be sure you check for condensation inside the container a few days after storing your herbs. If moisture is present, the herb wasn't completely dry, and you will want to spread it out on a window screen to finish the process.

General Instructions for Drying

The day *before* you expect to harvest, spray down the plants to clean dust and dirt from the leaves. The following day, cut the plant as early as possible after the morning dew has dried. Bundle the cut plants together at the bottom and tie with a string. Label them so you will know later what they are, and hang them upside down in a warm, shady location. Shelter from the wind.

Check the bundles periodically to be sure they are drying properly. A properly dried herb should be dry to the touch and should crumble easily. Strip off the dry leaves, leaving the damp ones until thoroughly dry. The leaves should remain as whole as possible to retain the maximum flavor.

Most dried herbs will last at least two years, but don't be concerned if you've just dried what looks like a ten-year supply—home-grown gifts are always appreciated and dried herbs will make delightful presents for your friends.

Drying Seeds

Unlike the procedure for leaves, here the harvest is done while the dew is still on the plant. This added moisture helps the seeds stick to the seed pod while handling. A change in the color of the seed generally means that it is ripe and ready for the harvest. Coriander, for example, will turn from green to light brown; fennel, from green to light-greenish tan.

Harvest by clipping the entire seed head into a pillow case or paper bag. Gently shake, beat, or rub the seed head by hand to remove the seeds from the stem. The next step is to get rid of the chaff. The process for this, known as winnowing, is done today just as it has been for centuries—by dropping the seeds from a few feet up in front of a breeze, letting the heavier seeds fall onto a sheet while the chaff blows away. You can do this outside on a day with a gentle breeze, or in front of a fan. If you have just a few plants to harvest, you can clean the seeds by hand.

10

After winnowing, the cleaned seeds are spread out on a window screen to dry and fully ripen. The same precautions apply as in drying leaves: Avoid heat, light, and moisture. When the seeds are ready to store, they are relatively hard and dry to the touch.

Freezing

You have yet another option for preserving some herbs: freezing. After harvesting the leaves, the herbs are washed carefully and dried completely. The stems are then removed along with yellowing leaves and other extraneous matter. Carefully wrap in freezer wrap and place in the freezer to enjoy at a later date. A few favorites are: chives, parsley, basil, mints, dill, chervil, marjoram, oregano, rosemary, sage, savory, tarragon, and thyme.

We've gone to some length about the drying process to ensure that you understand what is important. Actually, the drying process is quite flexible, and you can try any number of things you feel may work. As will happen, it can rain for a week just after you've harvested your herbs. Don't be alarmed. Your herbs can be dried in a low oven, like basil. In any case, a little practical experience is the best teacher. The rules for home drying are not *that* hard and fast, so don't be afraid to experiment. You may even revolutionize the home-drying industry. Regardless, you're going to have plenty of herbs to work with and lots of time during the season to perfect your techniques.

Companion Planting

Higher Yields, Reduced Insect Damage — Healthier Plants!

While this could be an advertisement for the latest chemical insecticide, it very aptly describes the virtues of companion planting. Just as herbs traditionally have been used to prevent sickness in humans, likewise they can be used to keep your garden plants healthy. This role, in which herbs are used to protect or stimulate the growth of other plants, is known as companion planting.

Companioning was introduced by Mother Nature several millennia ago, but even so it is a fairly new subject in scientific circles. Scientific studies support the theory of companion planting; however, evidence relating to herbs as companions is only now being looked at seriously. Many naturally occurring symbiotic relationships have been studied in great detail. This symbiosis is most easily noticed in the desert, where groups of plants and animals live in small restricted communities, each plant or animal interrelating with the others by providing food, shade, water, or other necessities. Here the absence of even one of the members may be detrimental to the entire ecosystem.

As far back as early Rome and the medieval herbals of Culpeper and Gerard, enthusiasts have extolled the benefits of herbs as garden and orchard companions. However, the best and most practical proof of companion planting is seeing the plants in action.

The most common application for herbs as companions is pest control. The authors were amazed when they witnessed a southern Colorado garden that had been devastated by pests, while an adjacent herb garden was left virtually untouched. If the gardener had planted the herbs with the vegetables, he might have saved both his crops.

There are several theories as to why herbs are effective in this role, with the most popular reasons centering on plant smell. Theory has it that strongly scented herbs so mask the odor of the protected plants that bugs cannot find them. Another possibility exists that bugs ravaging next to a strong-smelling herb find their dinner less than appetizing.

Further theorizing suggests that root exudations of companions build up in the soil. These soil "additives" may affect the eggs or larvae of the pests. If this is valid, it would then be wise to give your companions a few years' grace before passing final judgment as to their efficacy. It may take the herbs a couple of seasons to build up enough repellent to be effective.

Other reasons for companion planting are: increased yields in some plants and better pollinization from beneficial insects attracted to certain herbs. Borage and lemon balm, for example, attract many bees, and hyssop is noted for its ability to increase the yield of grapevines when planted nearby.

It is difficult, if not impossible, to set out an exact ratio of companion to protected plants. It can even vary from year to year and garden to garden. The herb's influence must be felt by the plant to be effectively protected. If your pest problem is severe, strong herbal influence will be necessary, and you may need many herbs to protect just one plant. On the other hand, if your bug problem is slight, the herbal influence need not be as strong to provide adequate protection. Experimentation is the key.

There are several ways in which herbs can be planted as companions. In one method, the herb seed is mixed with the seed of its companion and planted in the same furrow. The ratio of herb seed to companion seed is determined by the extent of your bug problem. Sowing in this manner should produce an abundance of both plants. After germination the obvious differences in the young plants will minimize the problems in thinning back to accommodate your garden's particular needs.

Another way to companion plant is to create an herbal border around the plants to be protected. Many herbs, such as marigolds, sage, and basil, are perfectly suited to this task. A good example of this would be to completely surround your tomato plants with a border of basil, greatly reducing the chances of bug infestation. Marigolds or calendulas, the best-known bug wardens, could be planted around the perimeter of your garden, thereby shielding the entire area.

A third way to plant is to have beneficial herbs in the same vicinity. The case of yarrow is a good example, as it is said to enhance the essential-oil production of other plants. Many herbs, such as borage, coriander, and chives, are of general benefit because they attract pollinating insects such as bees.

The following Companion Chart is a combination of research, practical experience, and suggested pairings. It is interesting to note that several of these garden combinations are also found together in the kitchen. For example, basil not only grows well, but also goes well, with tomatoes. Likewise, savory stands by beans from soil to soup. The herb world is just now being rediscovered. This chart is by no means the final say, merely suggestions derived from practical experience and from many generations of gardeners. Experimentation in companion pairing is encouraged.

COMPANION PLANTING
GUIDE

BASIL & OPAL BASIL
are tender annuals especially liked by tomatoes and asparagus and aid in repelling flies and mosquitoes. Keep this annual far away from Rue plants.

BORAGE
The flowering "herb of courage" improves the growth, flavor and disposition of its neighbors. Plant near tomatoes to discourage tomato worms and with strawberries if it can be kept small by pinching back.

CARAWAY
A plant helpful in loosening heavy soil, Caraway likes peas and beans and dislikes crowding.

CATNIP
Plant this minty scented perennial as a border to repel flea beetles.

CHAMOMILE
"The plant doctor." Plant throughout your garden to improve the general health of plants. Set near ailing plants to give them a boost. A strong tea made of the entire plant (stems, leaves and flowers) used as a spray helps prevent a devastating fungus condition known as damp off.

CHERVIL
The "gourmet's parsley" can improve the growth and flavor of radishes. Intermixing the plants within a row is ideal. Radishes are harvested early in the season leaving the large, slower growing Chervil to take over the row as it matures.

CHIVES
Companion plant this perennial as you would onions. Try a border around your celery or carrot patch but remember Chives dislike peas and beans.

CORIANDER
Plant this aromatic annual throughout your garden to discourage cabbage moths and encourage pollinating insects. Coriander grows well with Anise.

DILL
can be closely planted with cabbage, lettuce, onions and cucumbers, but avoid the carrot patch.

FENNEL
An unsociable but beautiful plant, this feathery-leaved biennial is best when planted away from your garden entirely.

GARLIC
One of the companion workhorses. It will deter pests of all kinds when planted throughout the garden.

HYSSOP
A healthful, old-time herb said to increase grape yields when planted nearby. It also discourages both cabbage moths and radishes.

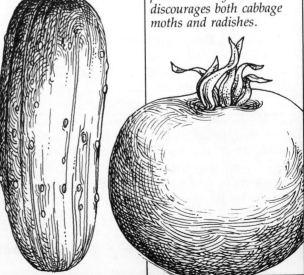

COMPANION PLANTING
GUIDE

MARIGOLD
This is a very famous flowering companion plant, discouraging many garden pests, particularly bean beetles and nematodes.

THE MINTS
Peppermint, Spearmint and Catnip when used as a protective minty border will help repel rodents. The mint family is also useful in keeping egg laying moths out of your cabbage patch.

NASTURTIUM
This useful plant helps deter aphids and squash bugs while making a flowering companion to cabbages and radishes.

PARSLEY
This friendly biennial will be a welcome border to your permanent tomato or asparagus bed. Onions and carrots also will thrive if sown near it.

ROSEMARY
This tender perennial plants well as a border to carrots, cabbage, Sage and beans.

RUE Liked by rasperries and roses, but disliked by Basil. The ''herb of grace'' repels flies and many other troublesome garden insects. It's good to plant Rue around manure piles and barns for its fly repelling qualities.

SAGE This healthful herb is an excellent companion to the cabbage family. It also brings vigor to carrots, and Rosemary, but will discourage cucumbers.

SUMMER SAVORY
The beneficial bean herb helps deter the bean beetle and is a friendly neighbor to onions.

TANSY A beautiful, fern-like, flowering border plant. Tansy will help keep ants and flying insects out and bring many compliments in. Plant under fruit trees to repel bores.

THYME Plant near cabbage to repel cabbage worms.

YARROW is an attractive perennial that helps make aromatic plant neighbors more potent. It is reputedly planted next to scented herbs to make them stronger.

Lunar Planting

At any given point throughout history, men have been at odds to define the magnitude of influence the moon has on the earth. Skeptics scoff just as adherents vehemently hail the importance of lunar cycles. This is as true today, as it was in the cradle of civilization. What we have today, however, is a broader perspective than ever before to view the information history has amassed. The evidence weighs heavily to equate the moon's importance with the sun's. As the moon swells the tidal seas, so it effects the cellular seas in every living thing. Minute tidal shifts, each rising and falling, build one upon the other to effect change. The migrating, spawning, and breeding habits of fish. Color changes in sea animals. The fertility cycle in women.
The quality of timber harvests. The mental attitudes of people. And, certainly the germination and growing characteristics of plants. For the skeptic, sowing herb seeds in relation to the waxing and waning phases of the moon is by no means vital to a successful herb harvest. There is, however, evidence to support lunar planting as a logical and effective approach to successful germination and growth.

The transition the moon makes through its various phases (new moon, first quarter, full moon, last quarter) corresponds to periods of plant growth and germination. Two facts will always remain constant: The full moon is the time of greatest growth, and the new moon brings about a time of relative rest. Plant growth is stimulated during a full moon for two reasons: The sun and the moon are opposite one another in relation to the earth creating a strong lunar pull and secondly, the brightness of the full moon adds additional light to the plants' day increasing growth. During the new moon, on the other hand, celestial positions have changed. The sun and the moon are together in the sky. Less light is exhibited an the lunar effect is lessened.

As the moon moves through its stages, each growing phase is the harbinger of the next. Periods of rest and activity alternate, just as dawn follows darkness and darkness follows day.

A chart may be helpful:

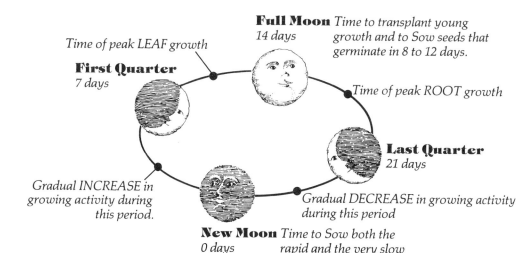

Full Moon *Time to transplant young*
14 days *growth and to Sow seeds that*
germinate in 8 to 12 days.

Time of peak LEAF growth

First Quarter
7 days

Time of peak ROOT growth

Last Quarter
21 days

Gradual INCREASE in
growing activity during
this period.

Gradual DECREASE in growing activity
during this period

New Moon *Time to Sow both the*
0 days *rapid and the very slow*
germinating seeds.

Seeds that germinate slowly, especially hard-coated perennials, do best when planted at the time of the new moon. In this way, the seeds that take over 21 days to sprout (Almost a full lunar cycle) have a chance to soak up water before a peak growth period provided by the emerging full moon. The seeds will sprout near the new moon, again bringing them into a prime growing phase.

Sow seeds with a medium length germination time (8 to 21 days) near the full moon. They can take advantage of the strong pull and the increased light of the moon during the seeds' crucial germination phase. Sprouting will occur near the new moon phase at a time when growth influence is beginning to increase.

Seeds that germinate rapidly (less than 8 days) do best when sown a few days before the new moon. Their quick growth allows them to sprout in time to enjoy the increased growth energies and activity as the cycle progresses to the full moon.

The idea basic to lunar planting: Have your seeds sprout near the new moon phase so they can take advantage of this time of new life and increased growth activity.

When transplanting, you can take advantage of moon cycles in the same way. Try to transplant near or immediately *after* the full moon. The decreasing lunar gravitational pull, with increasing earth pull and decreasing moonlight at this time, will stimulate root growth. The roots, which need special attention during transplanting, will receive a gravitational boost within the week following the full moon, preparing them for the period of relative rest during the week before the new moon.

Seeds sown with love and given care will thrive no matter when they are sown, but being aware of the basic lunar cycles may help you give them the advantage impetus provided by nature.

Planning Your Garden

Whenever herbs come to mind, one thinks of their medicinal and culinary uses, but another part of the rich history of these plants is their decorative aspect. Many herbs are grown today primarily for their beauty, their taste and medicinal value having fallen from favor in deference to form. Just as herbs come in a wide range of colors, shapes, and sizes, there are equally numerous ways to employ them to create an attractive garden or niche.

Perhaps the simplest use for ornamentation consists of planting a bunch here, a small border there, or a pot in the window—as the whim strikes, and you find a special place to show off each herb.

Yet another simple solution is to use large pots or planters, combining herbs that look well together and grow under the same conditions. This allows you to move your herbs where you wish; adding color and fragrance to the home when you're expecting company, gracing the entryway, or making a pleasing note on the patio. A small pot of chives and parsley may be moved from the kitchen to the doorstep as light varies, while a large pot with opal basil and sage will compete in color with any coleus you've ever grown.

If you want something slightly more permanent—without planning the classic herb garden—consider using cement blocks. Three hole blocks are perfect as an edge for the patio or a vegetable garden, and even more so when turned holes-up to contain a wide variety of herbs. You can even make a retaining wall doubly useful by stepping the blocks back as each row goes higher, filling them with dirt, and adding the herbs. Low-growing and creeping herbs are most attractive for this use.

The history of herbs is replete with religious and superstitious associations that make herbs an appropriate accompaniment to religious shrines, sundials, birdbaths, and garden and lawn statuary. Rosemary, for example, is customarily grown around shrines to the Virgin. A sundial may be adorned with a circle of calendulas. The Romans associated them with time, noting how they opened with the dawn and closed at sunset.

Herbs can even lend a fragrance to the path leading to the home or garden. Walks are a favorite place for plantings when used as an edging or in the cracks between the stones.

18

If, however, you want to go beyond these informal plantings, we've included a few traditional formal designs. The most popular of these is the knot pattern, a favorite since the sixteenth century. It incorporates three kinds of low-growing bushy herbs that can be trimmed to form small hedges. Thyme, lavender, sage, and hyssop are but a few that meet these conditions while providing a contrast in colors to emphasize the design. In this design, when one ribbon of herbs crosses another, it is trimmed slightly higher, with the lower hedge trimmed shorter near the crossing to exaggerate the knotlike pattern. Though plain rock or grass makes a handsome center for the knot, you may prefer a bunch of tall-growing or flowering herbs or even a sundial.

Another traditional herb garden, which may be formal or just a "happening," is the "gray" garden. Sage, horehound, rosemary, and many other herbs have a soft eye-appealing, gray-green foliage. Planted together, they act as a pleasant contrast to the brilliant green of the standard flower garden. A small gray garden, using primarily these herbs, could easily become the focal center of your plantings.

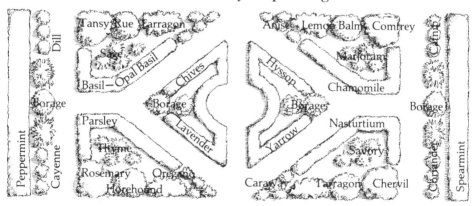

Other formal patterns can be devised: mazes, circles, wheels, rectangles, triangles—all are common. You can readily design your own, but take care that the tansy doesn't hide the thyme, and the borage can flower rather than be trimmed to a hedge. Use the creeping varieties where you need ground cover, and plant yarrow where its colorful flowers can be seen.

Herb garden possibilities are limited only by your imagination. Take advantage of rocks, natural slopes, terraces, and the multitude of colors, heights, and growth patterns, herbs can provide to create your personal herb garden. With just a little planning, you'll have a useful, colorful, and fragrant garden—adding a quality to your life that only plants can give.

The Herbs:

A Brief Introduction

From the time when primitive man first discovered that certain plants made his meat taste better or could ease his assorted aches and pains, herbs have been used as medicines and condiments. Just when this use began in time, we do not know. Records indicate that as long ago as 5000 B.C., the Sumerians used caraway and thyme as medicines. Egyptian papyri and archeological findings also show a wide range of herbs in use throughout the history of ancient Egypt, with their uses encompassing funerary rites and embalming.

The Chinese, too, had an extensive knowledge of herbs, with the best known of their ancient herbals supposedly being written around 2700 B.C. Though modern scholars suspect these writings actually date from sometime around the birth of Christ, the knowledge contained may indeed be as old as reported.

References to herbs abound in the Old Testament, with some of the earliest appearing in the Book of Exodus, which mentions hyssop and coriander specifically. Herbal references indicate that their use was widespread and commonly known at that time.

The Ancient Greeks seemed determined to write about herbs. Homer, who lived around 850 B.C., told of feeding parsley to horses. In the sixth century B.C., Pythagoras, best known for his triangles, postulated that anise might ward off epilepsy. A century later, Hippocrates, interested in herbs from a medical viewpoint, described over 400 remedies using herbs, over half of which are still in use today. Others followed: Aristotle, during the fourth century B.C., grew some 300 plants of medical value, and Virgil, in the first century B.C., grew herbs to entice the bees he raised.

The culmination of the Greek writings on herbs came in the first century, when an eminent physician, Dioscorides, wrote his *De Materia Medica*, which was to become the standard treatise on medicinal herbs for the following 1500 years.

A prominent Roman of the same century, Pliny the Elder, was hard at work on his 37-volume *Historia Naturalis*. This work and that of Dioscorides provided a fairly comprehensive picture of early herb uses. New Testament references support many of these writings, showing how commonly herbs were used.

During the Middle Ages, much of the authoritative information on herbs was retained in monasteries. For the general populace, herbal preparations were prescribed by folklore and superstition. Some worked; others were questionable but accepted.

The Renaissance brought with it a renewed interest in herbs as a subject for serious study, and this revival bore more fruit in England than elsewhere. Across a period of 125 years, a wide variety of books were published, beginning with *The Grete Herball* in 1526, a translation of a French work. From 1551 through 1562, William Turner issued the three installments of his even more popular *Herball*, followed by *The Herball or Generall Historie of Plantes*, offered by John Gerard in 1597. Gerard was a surgeon who gardened, but much of his knowledge apparently came from a Belgian work that he may have in fact plagiarized. Next to offer an herbal was Parkinson, an apothecary to James I, who published his *Theatrum Botanicum* in 1640.

All of these works were moderately scientific and authoritative, but by far the most interesting work of this era is Nicholas Culpeper's *The English Physician*, printed in 1653. Culpeper already had enraged the famous English College of Physicians by translating and publishing their Latin pharmacopeia, intended for doctors only, but his famous herb book went even further. Steeped in superstition and astrological references, it was an excellent source of both information and misinformation. By far the most readable and interesting herbal of the period, it described 369 plants, what to do with them, and how to recognize them, occasionally exploring the magic associated with them. Culpeper's book is still of interest today, though it somewhat taxes the reader to sift and sort fact from fiction.

During the centuries that followed, interest in herbs waned as new medicines were discovered and spices became generally available. Though many fine books were written, especially about the herbs found in North America, most did not gain the prominence they deserved. In the

1800's, use of herbs in medicine was revived in the form of patent medicines, which did little to enhance the reputation of herbs in the mind of the public.

It took World War I, when need of medications was great, to renew interest in the legitimate medical properties of herbs and to generate interest in growing them in any great quantities. From that surge of interest came the writings of Maude Grieve, an Englishwoman and Fellow of the esteemed Royal Horticultural Society. Her book, *Culinary Herbs & Condiments*, appeared in the 1930's and still is one of the best modern books on herbs. Though written for use in England, her cultivation instructions are so explicit that use is easily adapted to other parts of the world.

The current revival of interest in herbs began in the 1960's, when people were becoming disenchanted with artificial flavorings and synthetically derived medicines. Herbs are now common in kitchens, under the scrutiny of scientists looking for safer medicines, and are the subject of a large number of recent books. Evidence of herbs' usefulness has brought them to the forefront of thought, increasing an interest in growing them, and creating a demand for information on how to use them. Modern man has rediscovered herbs and found them to be everything the ancient Chinese and Greeks thought they were—and more.

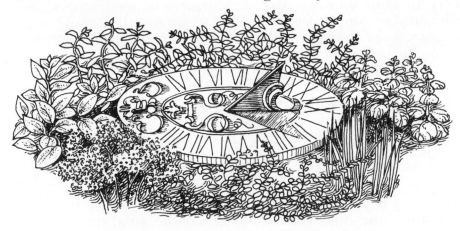

Anise

Pimpinella anisum Umbelliferae family

istorically, a view of anise takes on a perspective relative to its medicinal benefits, with the exception of a sixteenth-century use that is singularly minute and unique to this herb. Anise is the only herb ever to be grown in quantity to bait mice. Not at all earth-shattering, but for the sixteenth century, anise was apparently effective and a popular cure for an unpopular infestation.

Uses for anise date back at least to the time of Pythagoras, who, in the sixth century B.C., recommended holding the plant to ward off epileptic attacks. A century later, the father of modern medicine, Hippocrates, prescribed the herb for coughs, having noted it as an expectorant, a quality that is still appreciated today.

The Romans used anise for perfumes and flavoring, but the use most remembered was in *mustacae*—cakes prepared with anise and cumin seed that were eaten after lavish banquets. Although these cakes were served to prevent indigestion, their use is believed to have led to the tradition of serving cakes during large feasts, and may have been a forerunner of the modern wedding cake.

In 1305, anise was such a popular commodity in England that King Edward I placed a toll on it, in part to finance repair of the London Bridge. Three hundred years later, in the sixteenth century, Gerard recommended anise as a diuretic, carminative (a remedy for flatulence), thirst quencher, aphrodisiac, and cure for hiccups and halitosis.

Carminative and expectorant properties have been traditionally ascribed to anise, and modern usage concurs. In addition, its pleasing licorice-like flavor is often prescribed to disguise the evil taste in a number of medicines. Anise is used in baking, in flavoring soups, making anisette, Pernod and other liqueurs, and for flavoring livestock feed.

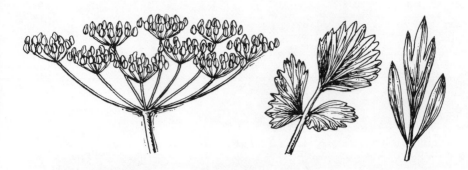

Description

Anise is unusual among herbs in that it grows two distinctly different leaves on a mature plant. The first leaves grown, near the base of the plant, are large and wide, with notched edges. Higher up the stem, the leaves are thin and feathery, leading to umbelled bouquets of tiny yellowish-white flowers in midsummer. The two-inch flower umbels produce seed that turns gray-brown in late August, at the end of the herb's growing season. The plant grows to be about 2 feet high, spreading out to 6 inches.

Care and Cultivation

Anise is a tender annual that must be planted each year if not allowed to reseed itself at the end of summer. Seeds are typically sown outdoors in the late spring, planted 1/4 inch deep in rows 12 inches apart. Light, sandy, medium-rich soil and full sun will ensure a good growth. The seedlings are thinned to 8 inches apart when 2 inches tall, and should be kept free from weeds. Do not transplant; the herb's long taproot is easily damaged.

Anise leaves may be harvested at any time. The seeds are harvested when they turn gray-brown by clipping the seed heads into a bag. Simply follow instructions in this book under harvesting seeds. Note that individual seeds or seed heads may mature before others. Harvest each as it matures.

How To Use Anise

Anise leaves and seeds can be used as a licorice-like breath freshener—and are simply chewed. The leaves are also used, though sparingly, in salads, over cooked vegetables, and may be steeped into a fragrant tea.

Springerle, the popular German Christmas cookies, take their flavor from the anise seed, as do some Italian cookies. Delicate cakes, soups, candies, cheese spreads, and applesauce all may be flavored using the seed.

In the garden, anise makes a good companion for its cousin, coriander.

Basil & Opal Basil

Ocimum basilicum Labiatae family

asil, or sweet basil, is one of the most commonly used herbs in the modern kitchen, ranking second in popularity only to oregano (a close relative) and parsley.

This is the "Royal Herb" of the French, assigned to the category of *"les fines herbes,"* and one of their traditional seven salad herbs. Even today the herb mixture *fines herbes* contains basil, lending its spicy, clovelike quality to this blend. Basil is respected worldwide for its individual flavor, enjoyed for its aromatic properties, and is universally indispensable as a seasoning for soups, salads, sauces, and ragouts.

Yet in the distant past, basil was verbally discredited, regarded as anything but indispensable, and in no way resembled the herb of love hailed by Keats and Shelley in the nineteenth century.

Early Greeks sowed the seeds of basil amidst rancorous shouts and vile curses, believing the herb would thrive under such conditions because of its affinity for evils and poisons. In so doing they may well have been among the first to believe that talking to plants would affect growth.

Legends abound associating the herb with the propagation of scorpions and

25

suggesting it as the cure if one is bitten by lizards and venomous beasts. For reasons known only to the ancients, scorpions supposedly thrived around basil plants, under pots planted with basil, and in fields of manure strewn with leaves of the herb. One French physician even claimed that scorpions would be born in the brain if one simply smelled the fragrant herb. Appropriately, his name was Hilarius.

Medieval tales tell of using the basil leaf as a remedy for being bitten or stung by a wasp or hornet. The leaf placed near the wound reportedly drew the poison to itself. The herbalist Culpeper, in the 1650's, reasoned that "Every like draws its like." When attitudes toward basil took a turn is not known, but ardent reverence was contemporary with disfavor.

Feelings for the herb in its native India have always run high. Pots of the sacred herb are grown in the temples, and homes built where basil grows are considered free from harm. Fresh sprigs of basil are even placed on the breast of the dead as protection on their journey into the unknown.

In the West, sentiment in favor of basil began to grow. Pliny defended it. The Greek physician Dioscorides took a moderate stand, prescribing small amounts with wine as good for the eyes. Parkinson, in the seventeenth century, recommended basil for sweet washing waters and nosegays. The Italians attached sentiments of love and affection to it. And with time, the strong aroma of basil became as familiar to the cooks and gardeners of Louis XIV as it is to French cooks today.

Description

There are many varieties of basil, but the most common and frequently used is sweet basil. The color variation of this herb, opal basil, is similar in most respects except that its foliage is dark purple, and the scent is not as pronounced. It's valued as an ornamental plant as well as a culinary herb. Opal basil is known also for its ease of culture under fluorescent lighting, making it an ideal indoor plant. Basil normally grows 18 to 24 inches high and spreads to a foot across. The leaves are generally lighter in color underneath, dotted with dark oil cells, slightly toothed at the edges, and soft to the touch. Whorls of white-topped pink flowers form at the end of each stem and bloom from June until the first frost.

Care and Cultivation

Both sweet and opal basils can be started, grown indoors, and later transplanted outside. But serious consideration should be given to cultivating them as indoor pot herbs. Basil is quite sensitive to frosts, which limits its growing season in many northern regions. Also, basil is at its best fresh, rather than dried.

Basil seeds can be sown annually outdoors in the early spring, well after any danger of frost. (You may even wish to revive the ancient Greek sowing techniques.) Soil should be rich, well drained, and in a select, but sheltered spot. Sow in rows 12 inches apart, covering with 1/4 inch of soil. The plants should be thinned to a foot apart when 2 to 3 inches tall. After thinning, the addition of a mulch will help control weeds and retain moisture. Starting indoors will assure larger plants earlier in the season. The seeds germinate easily in 5 to 10 days.

Basil is harvested fresh by pinching off single leaves or sprigs at stem ends when the plant has grown reasonably large. For drying, it should be harvested prior to flowering, leaving a node with at least two shoots to ensure further growth of the plant. Basil will continue to grow, providing you with an ample supply of the herb, both fresh and dried.

How To Use Basil

The most popular use of basil is in combination with tomatoes. It is a savory addition to nearly any tomato dish or sauce, and is particularly delightful when chopped fresh on sliced tomatoes. Basil can be used when preparing omelettes and other egg dishes, meats, fish, poultry, and stuffings. It provides a tasteworthy, attractive garnish to salads. Medicinally, when basil is brewed as a tea, it soothes nervous headaches, calms upset stomachs and was often prescribed as a tonic against rheumatic pain.

Borage

Borago officinalis Boraginaceae family

*T*he size, color, and overall appearance of the borage plant are striking enough to command that special corner of an herb garden. It's a good-sized plant, branching up 1-1/2 to 3 feet high and spreading out 18 to 24 inches. The round, branching stem is hollow and succulent, growing from a single taproot. Pointed, slightly oval leaves alternate up the stem and are about 3 inches long and 1-1/2 inches wide. Underneath, the leaves are veined, while on top they're wavy, and like the entire plant, they're covered with fine white hairs. From the top of the plant, clusters of buds and star-shaped flowers nod gently downward. Here the color varies from the soft greens of the leaves and stem. The small stems leading to the buds gradually turn dark red. When the buds flower, the petals reveal their beautiful violet-tinted blue and the prominent cone, formed by the black anthers at the flowers' center.

History and Uses

As far back as 23 A.D., Pliny, the Roman naturalist who authored the 37 books of *Historia Naturalis,* praised borage for giving courage, exhilarating the spirits, and driving away melancholy. Medieval writings, too, attest the ability of borage to give strength of heart, lend courage, and impart a feeling of joy. In popular use as late as the early 1800's, young borage sprigs were clipped and brewed. The fresh leaves added their cucumber flavor to salads too, and the flowers garnished meals and wines. Medicinally, borage was used to promote sweating, dispel fever, as a poultice, a purifying agent, and a diuretic.

28

Care and Cultivation

Before planting, remember that borage is considered a hardy annual. This means the plant will not live longer than one season. It can, however, reseed itself each year if the ground around it is left undisturbed. Initial plantings may be in fall or early spring. Seeds planted in the fall will winter in the ground and begin to come up as the ground becomes warm. Spring plantings will germinate in 7 to 14 days. Borage needs room—not a lot—but a good amount of space between plantings. Space according to the size guidelines mentioned earlier and sow thinly 1/4 inch deep in rows about 18 inches apart. When the young growth is 2 inches tall, thin to 15 inches apart. Borage does not respond well to transplanting. Sow your seeds where you'd like your plants. Seeds sown even in poor soil take well if the soil is slightly sandy to provide drainage. Plants flourish with moderate amounts of water and lots of sun. Borage grows rapidly and matures in about six weeks.

How To Use Borage

Because of its size, borage is often used as a border where it can be seen and where large plants are desirable. If kept small, it is a compatible companion for strawberry plants. The leaves are edible, with a light cucumber flavor. Best when picked before the plant flowers, the leaves can be

used to flavor salads, cooked as a green, braised with beef, or used in ragout. The blue star-shaded flowers usually are cut when fresh and make a delightful garnish in iced summer drinks.

They may also decorate cakes and ice cream and add their color to potpourris. The flowers may be candied by dipping them in egg white and then sugar. The dried leaves are often used to make a wintertime herbal tea. As a garden companion, borage is excellent in attracting pollinating insects.

Borage Tea

Start with 2 tablespoons of dried borage leaves or 4 tablespoons of freshly chopped leaves and add boiling water. Allow to steep for 3 to 5 minutes. Taste. Borage tea is normally mild. If the flavor is too mild for you try adding a sprig of lemon balm.

29

Calendula

Calendula officinalis Compositae family

Though the Latin species name *officinalis* indicated calendula had officially recognized medicinal value at the time it was named, this Southern European herb was not given prominent mention by herbalists until the Renaissance. Apparently, the calendula was well known, for many writers described it, listing uses for it that included headache, toothache, and jaundice. Culpeper thought it good for strengthening the heart and somewhat useful in combating smallpox and measles.

Calendula's golden-orange flowers decorated churches and church gardens during the Middle Ages, when the plant's common name, marigold, was also given as "Mary's Gold"—an association with the way the flowers were placed on the statue of the Virgin in the church. The name marigold attached to the calendula did not derive from this association, however, rather from the name of a similar plant, the marsh marigold. The religious connotation came later.

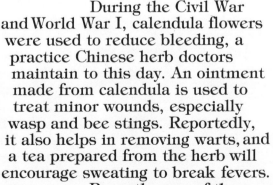

During the Civil War and World War I, calendula flowers were used to reduce bleeding, a practice Chinese herb doctors maintain to this day. An ointment made from calendula is used to treat minor wounds, especially wasp and bee stings. Reportedly, it also helps in removing warts, and a tea prepared from the herb will encourage sweating to break fevers.

Recently, one of the authors of this book was badly burned on the arm, and treated by a physician friend. Dabbling in homeopathic remedies, he used an ointment called "Golden Calendula." The burn healed rapidly —a pleasant introduction to the virtues of calendula, the pot marigold.

Description

Calendula opens its yellow-orange flowers to the dawn and closes them with the sunset—a daily summer ritual from June until the first frost. The numerous petals, radiating from a green button-flower center, identify the herb as a member of the family *Compositae*, which includes the chamomile and the ever-present dandelion. Long yellowish-green, bladelike leaves reach to 5 or 6 inches in length. The plant generally grows to a foot high and is accompanied by numerous leaves.

Care and Cultivation

Calendula is a tender annual. Start in warm, fairly rich soil with a sunny location. The seeds will germinate for only one year after they form, so be sure you get them from a recent crop. Germination takes 8 to 10 days, with even moisture and temperatures around 60° F. Thin to about 10 inches apart and keep free from weeds.

Only the flowers are harvested, and of those, only the petals are used. On a sunny day pinch off the flowers and remove the petals to dry in the shade on paper. Store in a tightly closed jar. The petals absorb moisture greedily, and moisture will lessen their color and flavor.

How To Use Calendula

Calendula petals are a standard substitute for saffron when color is desired and taste is less important. The sweet and salty taste of the flower petals adds interest to salads, where the herb is generally used fresh, and to soups, where the dried form is used.

Throughout the garden, calendula's flowers add a touch of brilliant gold that lasts from late spring until early fall, contrasting pleasantly with the colors of other herbs.

Caraway

Carum carvi Umbelliferae family

n the history of herbs, none goes back farther than caraway. Household remains suggest its use dates back to the time of the Neolithic and Bronze Age lake dwellers in what is now Switzerland.

Written records show it was enjoyed by the ancient Greeks, and it has been cultivated all over Europe since the Middle Ages. Shakespeare mentioned it as a popular herb of his day, and even today it remains in high esteem.

Grown primarily for its pleasing taste, caraway is also a minor medicinal herb. The ancient Sumerians mentioned it. Dioscorides, in first-century Greece, recommended it as a tonic for pale girls, and the Romans ate it to relieve indigestion. Twelfth-century German medical texts noted its usefulness, and both Culpeper and Parkinson recommended caraway as an antiflatulent—Parkinson thinking it would also warm the stomach and serve as a diuretic. Folklore credits caraway with stimulating the memory, and thus giving rise to its use in love potions and the feed of homing pigeons.

Today caraway is an important ingredient in foods ranging from breads and sauerkraut to a liqueur named Kümmel. Its oils flavor commercially prepared sausages and meats, and scent perfumes and mouthwashes. The seeds, which are high in fat and protein, are fed to cattle after the essential oil has been pressed from them.

Description

Caraway is a hardy biennial that survives winters even in Canada. Its feathery growth resembles that of carrots, as do its tapering roots. The first summer the plant grows to about 8 inches, and then reaches its final height of 2 to 3 feet during the following year. It produces white flowers in clusters, or umbels, the second summer. The fruit, which we call the seed, ripens in August.

Care and Cultivation

Seeds are sown outdoors in the early spring, planted 1/4 inch deep in rows 12 inches apart. Do not transplant. Thin by pinching, not pulling, to stand 6 inches apart when the young plants are 2 inches high. Control weeds with a mulch. Caraway does well in a heavy, dry soil (which it will loosen) and grows best in full sun.

Harvest the seeds as they darken and become ripe on the seed stalk that comes up the second year. If only some seeds are ripe, harvest anyway. The unripe seeds will ripen as they dry. Cut the full seed head and put it in a bag for several days to mature. Often, if the seed head is hung upside down in the bag, the seeds will loosen and fall, becoming separated from the chaff with little work on your part.

Leaves may be used at any time. If you wish to cook the roots, harvest them while still tender, early in the second year of growth.

How To Use Caraway

Caraway leaves are added to goulashes, stews, and soups, where they impart much the same flavor as the seeds. The roots are eaten as you would carrots or parsnips.

The seed is delightful with baked apples (one of its oldest uses) or in apple pies, and is a common ingredient in rye breads and sweet pastries, cakes, puddings, and cookies. Hot, buttered, sweet biscuits with caraway seed and raisins are perfect for a cold winter morning. It is added to potato and beet salads, cooking cabbage or sauerkraut, as are the leaves. Rub it on pork before roasting for a savory new taste. Pickled vegetables, especially beets, are improved by caraway-flavored vinegar.

As a companion plant, caraway is good with peas and beans, but keep it well away from fennel.

Catnip

Nepeta cataria Labiatae Family

wo types of catnip are commonly found in the United States. *Nepeta cataria* is the more familiar plant, 2-3 feet tall, and is seen throughout the country growing wild. *Nepeta cataria mussini* is a domesticated variety; a much lower-growing, bushier plant about half the size of the cataria.

Both plants have toothed leaves 2 inches long, and the square stem that distinguishes the mints. The leaves are soft, grayish-green, lighter in color on the under-side, and like the entire plant, covered with fine hairs that give a downy appearance. White-to-lavender flowers bloom on spikes at the ends of each stem in late June.

History and Uses

Originally, catnip had its roots in Central Europe, the temperate zones of Asia and Great Britain. Settlers coming to the Americas brought it with them and grew it in gardens, from which it quickly spread so that now catnip can be seen in a wild state growing in open fields and along waterways across the United States.

It was the British who first brewed and sipped catnip tea, long before trade with China brought westward the flow of teas from the East. Today catnip is grown as a culinary herb in France and parts of Europe, where the fresh shoots and leaves impart their lemony-mintness to everyday cooking.

The principal use for catnip, however, sets this herb apart from all the other herbs. Its single most popular use is to delight one animal. The cat. Whether tabby or tiger, catnip causes even the most aloof feline to shed its dignity, roll, pounce, preen, and wallow in fits of euphoria.

Care and Cultivation

When growing catnip, it's important to keep two things in mind—the cat and this old rhyme:

If you set it, the cats will eat it;
If you sow it, the cats won't know it.

To start your plants right, give them a permanent home in the garden. Though they can be transplanted, it's not advised. The oils expressed from handling young plants could easily attract any rambunctious cat within nose range and their desire is singular: early harvest.

Catnip is remarkably un-fussy, growing readily from seed, and is tolerant of most garden soils, even poor, dry soil. Like horehound, another *Labiatae*, it requires less water than other "mints."

The seed is sown in the fall or early spring by scattering thinly along a furrow 1/8 inch deep. Springtime germination takes about ten days. After the young plants have gained a foothold, thin to about 20 inches apart. When the buds appear, pinch back the tops of the shoots and the plant will become bushy, reaching out to about a foot.

35

Harvest your plants by cutting off the top leaves and flowers when the flowers just begin to open in the early summer. Harvesting includes the smaller top leaves and larger, more mature leaves. During a normal year, you can expect three such harvests before the plants begin to yellow in late August. Catnip is a perennial; if you cut the plant back entirely before the seeds drop in the late fall, it will come up again in the spring. In the spring, catnip roots can be divided and spread.

How To Use Catnip

Whether for tea or your cat, catnip is best when used fresh. It can be dried, however, using both leaves and flowers. Your cat will enjoy it either way without further preparation, but you can put it in a small, loosely woven bag to contain it for play. When preparing the tea from catnip, steep but do not boil. Catnip is believed to repel rats, possibly because it attracts cats, and therefore makes a good planting around grains you might be growing.

Cayenne

Capsicum species Solanaceae family

Capsicum peppers are the New World's contribution to the tongue-biting group of condiments called pepper. Centuries before Columbus, Central and South American Indians used the capsicums to flavor foods—both the sweet, mild species and the small, hotter variety. Columbus, who was looking for black pepper, among other spices, found the capsicums to be superior in hotness and introduced them to Europe in 1493. Spaniards and other Europeans agreed that Columbus knew a good thing when he saw it, for by 1650 the peppers were grown nearly everywhere in Europe.

The group of peppers called capsicums consists of a number of species and an almost infinite variety of hybrids. They produce flavorings ranging from the mildness of sweet bell peppers and paprika, through the chilies so loved in Latin American cooking, to cayenne, the hottest of all. Plants vary greatly in size and the type of fruit they produce, with soil and weather affecting changes in the flavor inherent in

36

each. All have a typical sweetness with varying degrees of zest. In general, the smaller the pepper pods produced, the hotter they are. What actually varies is the amount of capsaicin, a crystalline substance, which seems more prevalent in small, thin-skinned peppers.

Care and Cultivation

Cayenne seeds are sown inside in the early spring, outside in late spring. Plant 1/4 inch deep in rows 30 inches apart, in sandy, rich, well-drained soil that is exposed to full sun. Thin to 18 inches apart when 2 inches tall. Plenty of water is needed in the early growth stages, but later hot, dry weather is favored. Cayenne requires the hot days to ripen the pepper pods, so an inside start is preferred in northern climates to lengthen the growing season. Cayenne transplants easily just like its cousin, the bell pepper.

Description

Plants grown for cayenne are nearly always annuals, though some species are perennials. They grow 2 to 3 feet in height, with some varieties ranging upwards to 6 feet. The plants vary as to the number of flowers. Most produce one or two whitish flowers where the leaves branch from the stems. These generate the pods which may vary in length up to 4 inches. The pods are elongated and turn fiery-orange to red when ripe.

How To Use Cayenne

After the peppers are ripened, the pods are harvested by pulling up the entire plant before the first frost. It is hung indoors to dry. If individual pods mature faster than others, they may be harvested as they turn red. When dried, the pods are finely ground and stored. Taste-test your cayenne, if desired. A milder seasoning can be obtained by removing the seeds from the pod before grinding.

The ancient Mayans used capsicums to cure cramps and diarrhea. More recent herbalists have recommended cayenne as a stimulant. Its primary use is to add a sweet, zesty flavor to soups, sauces, eggs, and meats. It may be used to make a pepper sauce and small amounts give homemade noodles a special flavor appeal.

37

Chamomile

Anthemis nobilis/Matricaria chamomilla Compositae family

ny discussion of chamomile is confused by the fact that at least two different plants are called by that name: *Anthemis nobilis*, called Roman chamomile, and *Matricaria Chamomilla*, the German chamomile. Both plants are similar in appearance, have comparable medicinal virtues, and grow so readily they tend to escape gardens to become weeds. It is surprising, then, to find that throughout the written history of herbs, authors have feuded about which, if either, is superior to the other.

Many English-speaking herbalists contend that the Roman chamomile is the "true" chamomile, while Germanic authors praise theirs as the better plant. The name-calling once went so far that the English herbalist Culpeper called German chamomile a "hateful weed," though he, like others, had to admit it had nearly the same virtues as the plant he extolled. The argument still goes on, extending even to whether or not an "h" is correct in spelling the herb's common name.

Historically, both varieties of chamomile have been used to make the pleasing, apple-scented teas which soothed the nerves and acted as general tonics. Dioscorides and Pliny, who didn't differentiate between the plants,

recommended chamomile poultices and baths as cures for headaches and for liver, kidney, and bladder problems. Culpeper prescribed chamomile tea for "cold and weak" stomachs, and the more contemporary English writer Maude Grieve lists the herbs as sedatives, carminatives, and tonics.

In Spain, chamomile is called manzanilla and gives its name to the very dry sherry produced near Jerez.

Description

Both forms of chamomile are similar in that they have much-divided, feathery leaves and daisylike flowers, white with a yellow button center, marking them as members of the sun-loving *Compositae* family, which includes sunflowers, dandelions, and calendula. German chamomile, which grows erect, reaches a height of 20 to 30 inches. The Roman variety grows as a ground cover, and may have occasioned the common name of the plant, derived from the Greek for "ground apple."

Care and Cultivation

Though Roman chamomile is a perennial that may be started from runners, it grows from seed in a manner similar to the annual German chamomile, described here.

Seeds are sown outdoors by sprinkling and pressing into the soil, which should be sandy and well drained. The seeds' potency rapidly diminishes, and use should occur within a year. Full sun and even moisture, which are required for a good growth, will also help germination, which takes 7 to 14 days. Thin or transplant to 6 inches apart when one inch tall.

Harvest the flowers while in full bloom, and keep the flowers well cut back to encourage new growth. The flowers are used fresh or dried.

How To Use Chamomile

Chamomile tea is prepared from the flowers of either plant, though the German chamomile has a milder flavor. The tea is sipped for pleasure, to soothe, or as a tonic. Chamomile flowers are often combined with other herbs in herb teas, where their flavor and pleasant effects are not obscured. The flowers can also make a cleansing facial steam or a hair rinse that lightens hair, especially highlighting blond hair.

In the garden chamomile plants improve the general health of all plants so much that they are nicknamed the "plant's physician." A fluid extract prepared by boiling the entire plant is believed to prevent damping off of seeds and seedlings when applied in a spray.

Chervil

Anthriscus cerefolium Umbelliferae family

hervil is a low growing annual with delicately cut, light-green leaves. The cooks' reference to chervil as the "gourmet's parsley" stems from its similar but more delicate taste. Unlike many herbs, chervil is generally not thought of as an herbal remedy. It was, however, mentioned by Pliny, who added it to his long list of plague preventatives. It also appears to have been used externally to soothe rheumatic pains and heal bruises. One traditional use which survives is chewing it for a case of hiccups. Primarily, chervil continues to be used to tempt the taste buds.

Description

Chervil is a hearty annual that prefers the warm days and cool nights of early spring and late fall. The 1/4 inch sticklike black seeds resemble those of the common marigold. Chervil grows 8 to 18 inches tall, appearing

as a delicate sister to its relative, parsley. The leaves are finely cut and somewhat lacy in appearance. The seed stem or umbel emerges from the center of the plant and is crowned by a palm of tiny white flowers. The delicate tuberlike root system is easily damaged, so transplanting and close cultivation are not encouraged.

Care and Cultivation

Chervil adapts well to indoor or outdoor growth. The seeds should be planted in the early spring as soon as the ground can be worked. A partially shaded location is best. Press the seeds into the bottom of a one-inch-deep furrow. Do not bury, since the seeds need light to germinate. Sprouts should appear in 10 to 14 days. Thin to stand 4 to 6 inches apart when the plants reach one inch tall. Keep moist for fastest growth.

Harvest the bottom leaves of chervil as needed and keep the center stem trimmed back to encourage new leaf growth. The entire plant can be cut back to one inch about 90 days after planting. A successive planting in early August will ensure a fresh supply for the fall.

Keep your dried chervil in a tightly closed container and out of the light. Without these simple precautions, it will yellow and go stale rapidly, as will parsley.

How To Use Chervil

Chervil is best used when fresh picked from the garden. Its delicate flavor enhances light summer salads and soups of all kinds. When used as a seasoning, chervil is usually combined with several other herbs because of its tendency to enhance flavors. To some, chervil is the herbalists' MSG.

Chives

Allium schoenoprasum Liliaceae family

The chive is not unlike the gypsy. It's known, yet it's unknown. It has its dark side. The hint of mystery. Indispensable for centuries, information easily substantiates its use as a culinary herb gracing both the gourmet and the common kitchen. Yet within the old herbals are suggestions of medieval witchery and healing. Gathered together in bunches, chives that hung from ceilings would ward off illness, and were probably even thought to dismiss the plague. There are hints of wound healing and medicinal preparations that relieved the digesting of heavy food. Chives were even involved in fortune telling. Like the gypsies, their origin is in question. Some say chives originated in China, but others believe they're rooted in Northern Europe; a few even suggest they're indigenous to North America as well. Few specifics are forthcoming, though records show the Chinese used and enjoyed the herb 5,000 years ago.

Regardless, their popularity is world-wide. The reason for this may be their mildness. Unlike the other alliums, onion and garlic, chives won't overwhelm you with their flavor. Rather, they are subtle, lending a delicate oniony taste to dishes that are enhanced by their brilliant color.

In addition, chives are one of the easiest herbs to grow, a satisfactory introduction for the beginning gardener. Their small size makes them ideal for growing in a special, sunny nook of the kitchen, where they can be clipped right into the cooking pot.

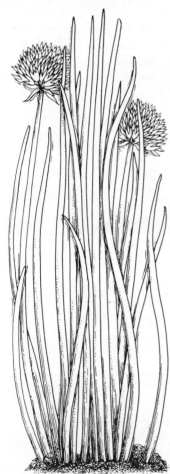

Description

Chives are distinguished by their spearlike leaves and ball-shaped flowers. The color contrast within the plant spars the pink-purple flower with the bright green, gracefully tubed leaves. The striking simplicity is reminiscent of an Oriental setting. The plant will grow to about a foot high, multiplying leaves in clusters spreading out to 6 inches wide. A dense thicket of leaves will come up year after year even in cold climates.

Care and Cultivation

Chives can be started easily from seed. Indoors at any time. Outdoors in early spring. Plant 1/4 inch deep, tapping fine soil over the seeds. Place 1 inch apart, in a well-drained, moist soil located in full sun. The seeds will germinate in 2 to 3 weeks if given even moisture. Plant within a year to be safe; seeds lose their potency quickly. Thin to 6 inches apart when 2 inches tall, and transplant outdoors.

Harvest by cutting the leaves close to the ground when the plant has become established. Continual harvesting ensures good growth and fresh, tender leaves. Harvest prior to blooming for maximum flavor, or while in bloom if you prefer a very mild taste. The leaves may be dried, but they are best when fresh or frozen.

Comfrey

Symphytum officinale Boraginaceae family

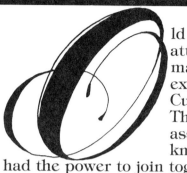

ld herbalists attributed wondrous cures to many herbs, but their tendency to exaggerate reached its peak when Culpeper described comfrey. The herb was long believed to assist broken bones in knitting—but Culpeper thought it also had the power to join together two pieces of flesh boiled in a pot!

If such miracles were indeed expected of the plant, disappointment was sure to follow and certainly such writing obscured the actual medicinal value of comfrey. A sad thing, for comfrey has been shown by modern science to be high in vitamins A and C, in phosphorus, potassium, and calcium, and in a number of trace minerals. It is one of the few vegetable sources of vitamin B_{12}, making it a

valuable addition to the diet of a vegetarian. It also contains allantoin, which has been found useful in treating ulcers, wounds, and burns.

Comfrey is again coming into popularity as a garden herb, and has been found useful in feeding livestock. Though most domestic animals have learned through the years to prefer other feed, they will eat comfrey and seem to benefit from it. One particular advantage is that it is a very hardy and prolific plant. Increasingly, too, comfrey is finding its way into herb teas and coffee substitutes, and the leaves are being enjoyed as a vegetable.

Description

Everything about the comfrey plant bespeaks its robustness. It is large, growing 2 to 3 feet high, with a sturdy, angular stem from which sprout in profusion very large leaves (up to 10 inches long). The leaves are wide, taper to a point, and are covered with small hairs which will make you itch if brushed against. Curving flower spikes bend as they bear comfrey's blue flowers, and bloom from late spring until the first hard frosts of winter.

Care and Cultivation

Few have successfully started this herb from seed, so comfrey is normally started from root cuttings. Generally the larger the cutting, the larger the plant. Recently a variety of the herb, which can be seed-grown, has been developed in England. This is a major breakthrough, but the seed is scarce and fairly expensive.

When starting with cuttings, bury them up to 6 inches deep in rich soil that is heavy with limestone. Place in a horizontal position, 3 feet apart in all directions. Weeds should be kept in check, either by weeding or with a mulch. Once the cuttings are established, they can be divided again when you want to increase the size of your comfrey bed.

To harvest, the plant is cut back, when it's one foot to 18 inches high, leaving at least 2 inches of stem. This is done just before the plant blooms, usually starting the second or third year. Harvest the first year for a large plant.

Comfrey is a very hardy perennial once established, surviving the severest winter. You may, in fact, have trouble getting rid of it. Even a small part of the root left in the ground will start a new plant, something to consider if you decide to move it elsewhere.

How To Use Comfrey

The fresh, tender comfrey leaves are treated like spinach, used in salads or boiled as a vegetable. Dried leaves, when ground, are often added to enrich homemade breads. The root, roasted and ground, can be added to chicory and dandelion roots as a coffee substitute. Brew the same way. If you intend to feed comfrey to livestock, remember they may prefer other feed, so give it to them when they are hungry. They will benefit from its vitamins and minerals just as we do.

Coriander

Coriandrum sativum Umbelliferae family

oriander is one of the oldest-known herbs. It was cultivated by the Egyptians several centuries before Christ, and was used for funeral offerings.

The Book of Exodus describes the miraculous food, manna, as being not unlike coriander seed.

The ancient Chinese thought it could bestow immortality, the Romans ground it to preserve meat, and fifth-century Greeks used it medicinally.

Its lot was drawn from the very beginning when coriander found its way into food. A world of food, in fact. The Europeans favor it to decorate and flavor breads and pastries. They also use it in distilling several liquors, including gin. It is an important ingredient in Indian curries, and its leaves are used in soups from Peru and Egypt. The seed is commonly used in the United States, both in pickles and sausages. The Chinese prefer it with vegetable as well as meat dishes. Essential oils of the coriander seed are used to scent perfumes.

The name coriander derives from the Greek *koris*, meaning "bug." Indeed, coriander attracts beneficial insects in profusion.

Description

Coriander, chervil, and parsley are all related, being within the *Umbelliferae* family, and coriander will take on some aspects of each as it grows, finally defining itself as individual. Plants will grow to be 2 or 3 feet tall, each slender branch displaying finely divided and delicate leaves. Pale mauve flowers appear in bunches, or umbels, at the end of branches, and forming

45

in midsummer, followed by green, round seeds that ripen in the fall.

Care and Cultivation
Coriander is a tender annual, growing from seed to flower in a single year. It's best when grown outdoors but may be cultivated inside if you like large plants. Because it is frost-sensitive, sow the seed as the weather warms and plant in a rich, dry soil in full sun. Planting the seed in small clumps is best; coriander stalks are slender and easily blown down by the wind. Plants grouped together will support each other. The coriander roots are too delicate to withstand transplanting, so don't. Young plants should be mulched lightly to keep down weeds.

How To Use Coriander
Any cookbook will supply you with recipes calling for coriander. Recipes for baked goods often require the seed, as do recipes for sausages and many meat dishes. Indian curries and Mexican dishes frequently include it.

The plant is a good garden companion to anise, but should be kept well away from fennel. Coriander discourages cabbage moths, but attracts many beneficial insects to pollinate your herb patch.

If you're harvesting for seed, a note. Plan to store coriander seed immediately after drying rather than using it. Often it has an unpleasant odor when just harvested. This dissipates as the seed dries, and the flavor continues to improve for some time in storage.

Dill
Anethum graveolens Umbelliferae family

nce dill was a cauldron herb, bubbling together with mystical ingredients in a blend that ancient sorcerers and magicians used to cast spells. It also hung in doorways, where it could ward off the evils of witchery, and its steamy vapors soothed and cured the fifteenth-century hiccup.

Today, dill gives us the advantage of both its leaves and fruit (seeds) as flavorful food ingredients.

Grown for each, it also is cultivated extensively for its oils, which, in distilled form, make it popular for commercial use in flavoring foods, not the least of which are cucumbers.

Description

Dill closely resembles fennel, sharing the same family, but is differentiated by its shorter, thin, feathery leaves. Its single stem reaches a height of 28 to 40 inches in late summer, when it is topped with lacy umbels of small yellow flowers. The seed that follows in the early fall is light gray-brown in color, flattened, and oval in shape.

Care And Cultivation

Dill is a hardy annual. It will grow readily in almost any climate if sown thickly in midspring and covered with 1/4 inch of fine soil. It prefers a sunny location and a well-drained, nonacid soil. Seed germination will take about 7 to 14 days, after which young plants can be thinned to 8 inches apart, when 2 inches tall. Though dill will not transplant well, be ready for the best—dill is not a hard plant to grow. Plant growth is rapid, often taking as little as two months to maturity.

Harvest the leaves from the young plants before the plant flowers, cutting close to the stem. Leaves dried in 2 to 3 days will retain maximum flavor; a low oven can be used if necessary.

The seeds can be harvested when the lower part of a seed cluster is ripe. It's not necessary to wait for all the seeds to ripen before cutting; the seeds will ripen as they dry. Cut the seed head and hang in the shade to dry or follow instructions for drying in this book. If the seed head is not harvested promptly, the plant will reseed itself with ease.

For pickling use, flowering clusters and a few leaves are taken, or occasionally a green seed cluster.

How To Use Dill

Aside from its use in pickling, dill makes a tangy, tasty addition to fish stews, sauces, dressings, and breads. Either the leaves or the seed are used, and some- times both. The leaves are also good freshly chopped and sprinkled

47

over salads and soups. A dill vinegar may be made by soaking either the leaves or the seeds in cider vinegar for several days.

The French use dill in sweet pastries, producing a flavor not familiar to most Americans. Try a French recipe. You'll discover that dill blends with sweet as well as sour tastes.

In the garden, cabbage, lettuce, onions, and cucumbers all benefit from being grown near dill, which later will enhance them on the table.

As a medicinal herb of long heritage, dill is still considered a carminative and stomach relaxer. Mild extracts can be made by brewing teas, as well as by the use of the essential oils in physician-recommended dosage.

Fennel

Foeniculum vulgare Umbelliferae family

For some, the generic goodness of herbs may be hard to see in an herb that initially appears to have negative traits. The case in point: fennel. Of the several types of fennel, its best growing companion is itself. Fennel is an outcast.

At times, fennel interferes with neighboring plants, and when it doesn't, they disturb it. If fennel is planted near dill, for example, the closely related plants will cross-pollinate, and the qualities of both will be reduced. As a general rule, it is best kept alone and entirely away from the garden. Bush beans, caraway, tomatoes, and kohlrabi are all adversely affected. Coriander, on the other hand, will prevent the fennel seeds from forming, and if wormwood is planted even 4 feet away, it can affect the germination and stunt the fennel's growth.

So the question arises, Why plant it?

History and Uses

Aside from its peculiar likes and dislikes, fennel is probably one of the more important herbs. Principally native to Southern Europe and the Mediterranean, fennel's long history winds back to the very dawn of civilization. Fennel and its seeds were originally used as a condiment by

Eastern Indians, Egyptians, and the Chinese. It was cultivated for its succulent shoots and aromatic properties by ancient Romans, and because of its restorative qualities was one of the nine sacred herbs of Anglo-Saxon England. Until recently it has been used medicinally as an antiflatulent and appetite depressant.

Today fennel is valued chiefly for its seed, which is its fruit. Grown commercially in India, Argentina, and Bulgaria, fennel is sold all over the world. The slightly curved, grayish-green seeds are fragrant and have a warm, sweet taste that's similar to that of anise. Fennel seeds flavor sausages, soups, breads, and pastries, sweet pickles and fish. The leaves are used as a garnish, for flavoring salads, and when finely chopped, enhance delicate sauces.

Akin to the common-garden and wild fennel is finochio or Florence fennel (*F. vulgare dulce*). This plant is a harvester's delight. It yields not only the spicy seeds and the greens to garnish, but grows from a base that closely resembles celery and is used as a vegetable. The long stalks which bear the leaves overlap at the base, forming a broad, pale-green or whitish bulb. This bulbous base grows to be quite large at maturity and is harvested and used as celery is used, either fresh or steamed with other vegetables.

the Outcast

Fennel.

Description

Fennel is a tall-growing (3-4 feet), thin-leafed plant, belonging to one of the most common herb families, *Umbelliferae*, and is similar to dill. Its stems are blue-green, while the foliage is feathery and bright green.

Planting and Growing

Sow fennel out-doors during the early spring in a slightly sandy soil. Plant 1/4 inch deep in rows of 12 inches apart. When the plants reach 2 inches tall, thin out to 12 inches apart. The method of harvest varies,

depending on the part of the plant
you want to use. To harvest the
bulb or stalk, wait until the base
has reached the size of a large egg,
or approximately 1 1/2-2 inches in
diameter. Pile soil around the base,
covering it above the ground. This
will blanch the base and stalks,
making them white and tender.
Harvest when the base has reached
4 inches and cut it off at the point
just above the roots.

F. vulgare dulce
FLORENCE FENNEL

If you have in mind
using seed or leaves, you cannot,
of course, harvest the base of all
your fennel plants. The leaves may be harvested for fresh use
a few at a time, or you may dry the entire top. The seeds are
harvested when they have just changed color and are dried.

Other Uses For Fennel

Along with the uses already mentioned, the seeds
alone can be chewed and will freshen the breath and act as
an antiflatulent. Boiled seeds reportedly increase mother's
milk.

Garlic

Allium sativum Liliaceae family

arlic is probably the
most frequently mentioned herb
in all the writings across the
millennia, and nearly everybody
says the same thing—it smells
awful, but it's good for you.

Its offensive aroma
turned it into the herb of the
common man—the man who worked and didn't care whether
his breath smelled bad from eating garlic, but who did care
that he was stronger for having eaten it. In fact, one of the
earliest recorded strikes was when Egyptian slaves refused
to work on the pyramids because they weren't receiving
garlic. This association with strength continued into the days
of Rome, when athletes in training ate it and the herb was
fed to fighting animals.

50

An impressive list of ancients believed in the benefits of garlic. Homer, Hippocrates, Aristotle, Theophrastus, Aristophanes, Virgil, Galen, and Pliny in their turn each praised the plant for purposes ranging from lending strength to harvesters (Virgil) to curing hydrophobia and being a laxative (Aristotle). In later years, though, Shakespeare thought the herb vulgar—after all, an actor should have sweet breath.

Legends surrounding garlic have abounded from ancient to modern times. One of the earliest was that it came into the world on Satan's left foot, with its cousin, the onion, on the right foot. It has been carried to ward off vampires, believed to prevent the plague, and credited with prolonging life. Bullfighters have carried it to keep bulls from charging, and it was used in India as a general protection against evil. Whatever might go wrong—garlic's unpleasant smell would keep it away!

Superstition and folklore aside, modern medicine has established that garlic is an antiseptic and may be useful in lowering blood pressure. There is even evidence that its strong aroma is offensive to insects, supporting old tales that garlic grown in the garden kept other plants free from pests.

Description

Garlic can be distinguished from any other plant by its smell, but it is also readily identified by its long, gracefully tapering, flat leaves and the white-to-pinkish flower clusters it produces in the summer. The bulb, when mature, is covered with whitish papery tissue that separates the segments, called cloves.

Care and Cultivation

Garlic is easily started by planting the cloves, about 6 inches apart and 2 inches deep, in nearly any kind of soil, though it prefers a moist, sandy soil. It needs lots of sun and a fairly long growing season to mature. Keep well weeded.

In warm climates, it is started in March for harvest in August. Colder climates dictate a later start, though you may start it early indoors and transplant later.

51

Harvest when the leaves begin to die back. Dig, and don't pull up the whole plant. Let it dry. Be careful not to injure the tops, as the bulb may rot, particularly in more humid areas. When dry, store, and use when needed.

Garlic sets may be purchased at nurseries or garden stores, but even garlic purchased in the grocery store generally will sprout with ease.

How To Use Garlic

Garlic complements almost every ethnic cuisine. It's often accompanied by parsley, which mutes garlic's strong flavor. Garlic's strength demands a subtle hand. Rub it on the sides of a bowl with salads. Try it in soups, with meats, in butter for garlic bread, and to accent any tomato dish. Garlic is even used in Swiss cheese fondue.

Though you may not appreciate garlic's rank odor in the garden, the surrounding plants probably will, for it helps keep them free from pests.

Horehound
Marrubium vulgare Labiatae family

I f you grew up in the days when a drugstore was still a store that sold drugs, you probably remember horehound drops and syrup as the sovereign remedy for coughs and colds. The cough drops are still around. In addition, our ancestors found many other uses for horehound. They drank it or applied it as a salve for poisons and the bites of insects, snakes, and mad dogs. It is native to the British Isles, and the Anglo-Saxons simply called it *hare hune*, "white plant." Their belief in its power against rabies gradually altered the pronunciation and spelling to the modern English name. The Latin name, *Marrubium*, really Hebrew, *marrob*, meaning "bitter juice." Horehound is one of the five bitter herbs that the Mishnah recommends for Jews at Passover.

The powerful taste makes it a little strong for a culinary herb. However, brewed into a tea, combined with honey or made into candy, it becomes unusually pleasant.

Description

Horehound is a bushy plant, a foot or two high. The leaves, serrated ovals about an inch long, grow in opposite pairs along the stem. A downy white fuzz covers the whole plant, making the leaves appear woolly-white below, gray-green on top. From June to September tiny white flowers appear above the leaves in tight little burr-like whorls. Fresh horehound has a strange musky smell which disappears when it is dried.

Care and Cultivation

Plant the seeds a quarter of an inch deep in fine soil—indoors in early spring, outdoors later. The young plants, which should appear ten to twenty days after sowing, need even moisture. When they are about 2 inches tall, transplant to about nine inches apart. The mature plants will thrive in poor, dry soil and full sun.

Horehound is a hardy perennial, hardy enough to be a weed in some places. However, the flowers usually don't appear until the second year, and in harsher climates it is not a long-lived plant. Therefore, it is usually best to treat it as a biennial and to sow new seeds each year. Where horehound does survive the winter, it is a hearty spreader, rapidly claiming a good portion of the garden if not checked. It can also be propagated by cuttings and root division.

Harvest by cutting off the entire plant 3 inches above the ground before it flowers. You should be able

to cut it back two or three times in a season.

Use

Horehound is attractive enough to plant just for its looks; perhaps as a decorative edge to a gray or silver herb garden.

Tea can be made by steeping two or three ounces of fresh leaves—one ounce of dried leaves—in a pint of boiling water. To make cough drops, brew a strong tea, boil it down, add sugar —eight or so pounds to the pint— and some cream of tartar. Cook this as you would any hard candy. The same strong tea mixed with honey makes a good cough syrup. In the garden, bees make a superior honey from its nectar.

53

Hyssop

Hyssopus officinalis   Labiatae family

ssociated with purifying, hyssop was used by the ancient Egyptians to cleanse lepers and likewise, in the Old Testament, King David speaks of hyssop as a cleansing purgative. This use continued into New Testament times, as noted by John, who tells of a sponge soaked in vinegar and hyssop which was placed in Christ's mouth at the Crucifixion.

From these early uses, hyssop was regarded as a holy herb, and was used as a strewing herb on the floors of medieval churches, both for scent and its noted purifying powers. This reputation spread into the home where it was hung to ward off the "evil eye."

Even the name, hyssop denotes it as being sacred derived from the Greek *azob*, meaning "holy herb." The Hellenes gave the plant this name because it was often used to clean temples.

Gerard's herbal followed a lead that Dioscorides had established: The plant was too common to bore a reader with its virtues. Culpeper, on the other hand, provided a long list of ills it was supposed to cure, including coughs, jaundice, bruises, toothaches, ringing of the ears, and lice.

Modern herbalists point out that the hyssop of the Bible probably isn't the same plant as the hyssop that grew in Europe. They suspect the Biblical plant was a form of marjoram and may have had antiseptic powers not associated with the modern European hyssop. To herb gardeners, such discussion loses importance as they contemplate the gently curled leaf of this beautiful herb.

Description

Grown primarily for its ornamental features, hyssop is a beautiful addition to any herb garden. It is a compact, bushy plant that grows 18 to 36 inches high. It is decorated with lovely smooth, dark-green leaves, and in the summer, with beautiful stalks of blue, pink, or white flowers, depending on the variety.

Care and Cultivation

It is started from seed indoors in the early spring, or outside in the late spring. It prefers poor, chalky soil. Seeds are sown 1/8 inch deep and covered with fine soil. They should be kept warm and moist, which favors indoor starting. Germination is in 8 to 14 days. The plants are thinned or transplanted to 12 inches apart and mulched when they reach 6 inches high. They transplant easily. If the leaves are to be used, they should be harvested before flowers form, though they still retain much flavor afterward. At the end of the year, the entire plant is cut back. Drying is easy in a shady location.

Hyssop is a hardy perennial that makes an excellent hedge around the herb garden. After several seasons, a hyssop plant becomes woody, and should be replaced with younger plants to keep a hedge looking neat. A hedge may also be allowed to reseed itself, which hyssop does with ease.

How To Use Hyssop

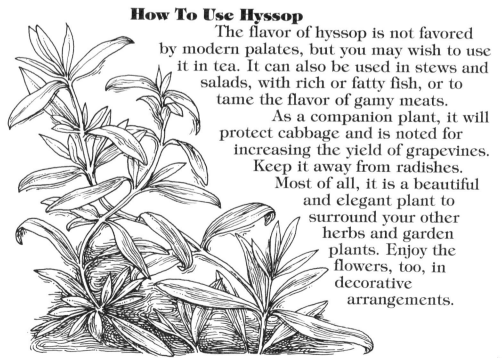

The flavor of hyssop is not favored by modern palates, but you may wish to use it in tea. It can also be used in stews and salads, with rich or fatty fish, or to tame the flavor of gamy meats.

As a companion plant, it will protect cabbage and is noted for increasing the yield of grapevines. Keep it away from radishes.

Most of all, it is a beautiful and elegant plant to surround your other herbs and garden plants. Enjoy the flowers, too, in decorative arrangements.

Lavender

Lavendula officinalis Labiatae family

mong the herbs known for their pleasant scent, none is better loved than lavender. The mere mention of the word brings to mind scented sachets and fragrant soaps. Interestingly its name derives from the Latin *lavare*, meaning "to wash." Washing with lavender-scented water and soap is just what people have been doing for several thousand years. The Romans and early Greeks bathed in lavender's marvelous fragrance with as much enjoyment as we do today.

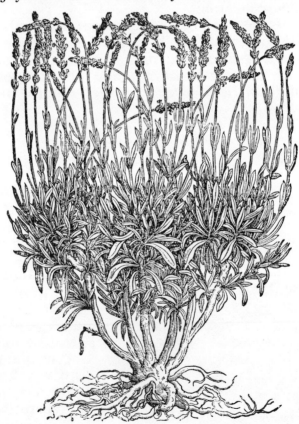

For a short time, however, during the Dark Ages, because lavender had no religious associations, was without superstition, and had few medicinal uses, it was relegated to relative obscurity. Interest in the herb wasn't revived until the late Renaissance, during a time when purely joyous things were more appreciated.

Foremost among lavender's medical applications was its use as an ingredient in smelling salts. Gerard, in 1597, wrote that lavender waters were helpful to those with palsy, and a century later it was believed to cure hysteria. Lavender water has been a centuries-old cure for sore throats, and its oil has been used to ease aches in joints.

More recently, lavender has been grown solely for its fragrance, and once you've enjoyed the sweet smell of a lavender plant, you'll need no other reason to grow it.

Description

There are a number of varieties of lavender. All typically grow to about 2 feet in height, bush out shrublike and are covered with narrow, gray-green leaves. In June and July, bluish, light-purple flowers form in spikes at the top of the plant, adding to the characteristic fragrance of the leaves. Varieties of lavender vary somewhat in flower hue, foliage color, and leaf width, but all are readily identified by the fragrant scent.

Care and Cultivation

Of all the herbs, lavender is one of the most difficult to grow. It's a tender perennial and temperamental. Light, chalky soil with full sun is best. Sow indoors in late winter or early spring, 1/4 inch deep. Germination will take 10 to 28 days, and will require even temperature and moisture. In the early summer transplant the seedlings outdoors, 2 feet apart, or into large pots if you wish to grow them indoors. Outdoor care will require a heavy mulch or protection where winters are cold.

Though lavender leaves are fragrant and useful, the flowers are the primary harvest. Cut them when they have just opened and the scent is the strongest. Dry on a screen in the shade.

How To Use Lavender

A potpourri is incomplete without the wonderful fragrance of lavender, and sachets or pillows of lavender lend a pleasing aroma to closets and rooms. Scented soaps are easily prepared at home, and like potpourris and sachets, make thoughtful gifts. Lavender leaves have even been used to stuff furniture cushions.

Planted throughout the garden, lavender will repel moths, just as it does indoors. Consider also using it as a beautiful aromatic hedge.

LemonBalm

Melissa officinalis Labiatae family

emon balm is easily recognized by the scent of its leaves, which have a heavy lemon fragrance when crushed. The leaves are light, yellowish-green, heart-shaped, with heavy veins and scalloped edges. Similar to mint, the leaves grow in opposing pairs up a square stem. Tiny bluish-white to yellow flowers nestle where the leaves join the stem, but are not numerous even in midsummer, and are often nearly hidden by the large leaves that bush out from the stem. The plant grows 2 to 3 feet high outdoors, about one foot high indoors, and is nearly as wide as it is high.

History

From the time of the early Greeks, lemon balm has been noted for the way it attracts bees. In fact, the scientific name for lemon balm is derived from the Greek word meaning "bee." This association has lasted through several centuries. Gerard thought that rubbing the herb leaves inside beehives would prevent swarming and would possibly attract additional bees to the hive.

Medicinally, lemon balm was prescribed by Dioscorides to be taken with wine against scorpion stings and bites of insects and mad dogs. Pliny agreed. In the 1500's, Gerard concurred with the ancients by saying lemon balm would close wounds and stings without causing inflammation. In later years the herb was credited with adding to longevity: Several Englishmen who habitually drank lemon-balm tea with honey reportedly lived to be well over a hundred.

Shakespeare mentions lemon balm as a strewing herb. However, its use was not limited to the floor. The herb's fragrant oils were commonly rubbed on furniture. Even today, the oils of lemon balm are used in making furniture polish and in perfumes.

Care and Cultivation

Lemon balm is a tender perennial that grows readily from root cuttings or seed. Like its close relatives, the mints, lemon balm is a voracious spreader and should be contained by a metal or wood edging. It transplants easily. In cold climates, it may be restrained by pots, which will simplify the move inside for the winter.

Seed is sown indoors in early spring, outdoors in late spring. Sow thinly in light, sandy soil, and cover with 1/8 inch of fine soil. Germination takes 12 to 20 days. Thin to 2 inches apart when the seedlings are an inch tall, then transplant to 18 inches apart when 4 inches tall. Lemon balm should be placed where it will receive full sun.

Harvest by cutting the entire plant 2 inches above ground. Dry quickly, in two days or less, at 90°F or higher. Lemon balm turns black if not dried rapidly. To retain the fragrant oils, handle gently while harvesting and drying.

How To Use Lemon Balm

Both leaves and stems of lemon balm are used, fresh or dried, to make tea. Steeping, up to fifteen minutes, for the maximum taste. Serve with honey. Fruit salads may be garnished with a lemon-balm sprig and the leaves are pleasant in many other salads as well. The leaves may be crushed or floated in fruit punches. Lemon balm will attract bees to pollinate your garden.

Marjoram & Oregano

Marjorana hortensis

Origanum vulgare Labiatae family

Any cook who uses both marjoram and oregano in the kitchen will know the two differ in taste and aroma. Botanists and herbalists, however, find these two herbs very confusing because of their similarity. To some, *O. vulgare* is not oregano, but rather wild marjoram. To others, marjoram is included in the genus *Origanum*, and thus is just another variety of oregano.

59

Though many agree that *O. vulgare* is oregano, they often mention another, smaller species as the *"true"* oregano; many assert this is merely a different variety of the same species and that both are equally good. Added to the confusion, there is Mexican oregano, also called Mexican marjoram. Neither is true; the Mexican variety is a different, totally unrelated plant.

In commerce, it generally is agreed that *M. hortensis* is marjoram, *O. vulgare* is Oregano, and Mexican oregano is labeled as Mexican oregano. But even here, there is a problem: depending on the market, marjoram may be sold as Oregano, or more likely, the opposite. Oregano is usually the more plentiful of the two, and thus generally cheaper.

If you're thoroughly confused, you're normal. The truth is: Similar as they may be, they are different and can be told apart. Marjoram is the sweeter-smelling and tasting of the two; oregano is the more robust in both its growth and flavor.

Although oregano is the favored plant for medicinal uses, both have been used since classical times in comparable ways — traditional uses include headache and toothache cures, and aids for indigestion and rheumatism.

Marjoram was a common strewing herb throughout Europe, and was also used as a magic charm against witchcraft in the superstitious Middle Ages.

Both herbs have been used to flavor food since the Greco-Roman era, with oregano's use probably dating back to ancient Egypt.

Though the herbs' flavors are similar, and in some cases interchangeable, clearly marjoram was the more popular of the two herbs until after World War II. When the pizza craze hit the United States, so did the "pizza herb." Demand for oregano increased by the late 1960's to nearly 6,000 times what it was prior to the war. But this increase wasn't brought about by pizza alone. The new found popularity of Mexican food must be included.

OREGANO

60

Description

Marjoram is a low-growing, bushy plant, ranging from 9 to 12 inches in height. Its leaves are narrow and small—1/8 inch long—and gray-green in color, with a downy fuzz that makes them appear even lighter green. In the summer, tiny "knots" of leaves and white-to-pink flowers form at the stem ends.

Oregano is a sturdier plant, generally growing about a foot high and creeping out to spread even wider. The leaves are larger and darker green than marjoram's. They're rounded, and come to a blunt point. Flowers form in the summer in bunches at the stem ends, in colors ranging from white and pink through blue and purple.

Care and Cultivation

Both marjoram and oregano are started easily from seed, either indoors in the early spring or outdoors in the late spring. Sow thinly in relatively rich, well-drained soil in full sun, and cover with 1/8 inch of fine soil. Germination takes 8 to 14 days and is followed by thinning when the plants become 2 to 3 inches tall. The seedlings should be kept well-weeded. Both herbs transplant easily.

When marjoram flowers the first time, cut back to 2 inches from the base. The second growth is the main crop, coming up much bushier. It, too, is cut back and dried in the shade. Leaves are stripped from the stem when dry.

Oregano is harvested by cutting back the center of the plant before flowering, which encourages fuller growth as well as providing the first harvest. Individual stems are cut before flowering and hung to dry, either in the sun or in the shade.

Technically, both marjoram and oregano are perennials. Marjoram, however, will not survive any but the warmest winters, so for practical purposes, it is grown as a hardy annual instead and re-seeded each season. It can also be kept indoors as a potted plant. Oregano, while a bit hardier, is treated as a tender perennial. With cover and mulch, it will survive moderate winters.

MARJORAM

61

How To Use Marjoram And Oregano

Marjoram is the ideal herb for the beginning cook—it can be used in almost any soup, sauce, stuffing, or stew, and goes well with any kind of meat. The general rule is: When in doubt, add marjoram.

Oregano is not quite so versatile, but goes well in any tomato dish, especially when accompanied by basil, and is required for many Italian dishes. The Mexican variety is *mucho fuerte* and its flavor stands out even in such strongly spiced dishes as chili con carne.

In many dishes, marjoram can be substituted for oregano, and sometimes the reverse is true, but use oregano more cautiously than you would marjoram.

TheMints

Mentha piperita/Mentha viridis Labiatae family

The mints—strong in scent and popularity! There are dozens of varieties, and all are easily grown, hardy perennials that spring up year after year. Two of them, however, edge out the others in popular regard—peppermint and spearmint.

History and Uses

The genus name for peppermint and spearmint, *Mentha*, comes from a mythological nymph, Minthe. Her love for Pluto sufficiently aroused Persephone's jealousy to warrant transforming Minthe into a plant. Minthe, the nymph, has nearly been forgotten, but the wonderful mint plants are foremost in the minds of most herb gardeners.

Throughout history its appeal has been universal, due, perhaps, to its versatility and cool fragrance. It has been a useful medicine since the early dynasties of China. Roman physicians recommended it to stir the appetite, as did Gerard, some 1500 years later. Culpeper, in the 1600's, noted nearly forty different ailments that mint was supposed to remedy. Though some of the herbal benefits he listed are derived from folklore and superstition, many of the medicinal virtues of mint have been substantiated. Remarkably popular throughout history as a medicine, today mint is officially recognized by pharmacologists as a carminative and local antiseptic. It is also used to mask the unpleasant tastes of modern medicines and to flavor pseudomedicines, such as mouthwashes.

The mints helped in their own way, too, to lighten the burden of the Dark Ages; leaves were often strewn on church floors, where the scents they released when bruised obscured the less than pleasing odors of medieval European living. In India sprigs of mint traditionally have been hung in rooms to freshen the hot, heavy air of that tropical climate. Logically, mints have found their way into potpourris and sachets right up to modern times—their clean fragrance a welcome addition to stuffy closets and stale rooms.

SPEARMINT   PEPPERMINT

Description

Mints are easily recognized as members of the family *Labiatae* by their square stems and opposing leaves, but varieties are difficult to tell apart; peppermint and spearmint are particularly difficult. Both plants have a similar dark green color, except for peppermint's slightly purplish cast. They both have pointed leaves with serrated edges, grow to the same height (18 to 24 inches), and are alike when they blossom, clustering lavender-to-violet flowers at the stem ends. Close examination, however, reveals that peppermint is petioled, its leaves connected to the stem by a small stalk. Spearmint, on the other hand, is sessile, and has no connecting stalk, growing its leaves right from the stem.

Catnip, horehound, and lemon balm are other members of the *Labiatae* family and are often called mints, though they are not true mints.

Care and Cultivation

Mints grow well from root cuttings. Any neighbor with a mint patch would be happy to share some with you. They are rampant spreaders if not controlled, but may be easily contained by using a metal grass edge or boards to prevent the lateral roots from wandering. Also, they may simply be removed and planted elsewhere, with little harm done to the hardy plant.

Mints grow easily in moist, rich soils anywhere in the world. Preferring some shade, they will grow amply in full sun. To grow from seed, sow 1/8 inch deep, barely covering with fine soil, and keep moist. Seeds will germinate in 10 to 20 days, after which you can thin the plants to 8 inches apart when they are 2 inches tall. Mints are slow to develop during the first year, but be armed to fight them back the second year. If your growing season is long, a light harvest may be possible the first year, but generally it is best to wait.

Usually, harvesting is done just before the plant blooms. Cut the entire plant to an inch above the ground. Remove any yellowed leaves on the remaining stem to ensure its health and continued growth. The prolific mints can be cut back two or three times a season, leaving plenty for fresh use, freezing, or drying.

A caution: Different varieties of mint should be planted as far apart as possible. True mints hybridize easily, cross-pollinating when in close proximity. The resulting hybrid combines the characteristics of both parent mints in a way which may not be favorable. If you plan to grow both peppermint and spearmint, starting them at opposite ends of the garden will maintain the integrity of each.

How To Use Mint

Peppermint and spearmint are different in taste but similar in use. Spearmint, being less pungent, is the more subtle of the two.

Both peppermint and spearmint are used as a stimulant, carminative, and stomachic. Peppermint combined with elder flowers and brewed into a tea is an old-time cold and flu remedy. Toothpastes and many breath fresheners are mint-flavored. You may even chew a leaf fresh from the plant to overcome the odors of onion and garlic.

Peppermint and spearmint are used to flavor candies and chewing gums. They are also used in sauces and jellies, or as a garnish for meats, particularly lamb. Some vegetables are enhanced by the agreeable taste of mint, the favorite being minted peas.

Mint teas are the world's most enjoyed herb teas, those made from mint leaves alone and those where mint leaves blend their cool taste with other ingredients.

Mints repel cabbage moths, which increases their value in the garden. Whether grown as companion plants or strictly as kitchen herbs, mints are an elegant and hardy addition to your herb garden, where they will be enjoyed year after year.

Nasturtium

Tropaeolum majus Tropaeolacae family

nless you're an experienced herb gardener, you probably think of nasturtiums as lovely, almost Oriental-looking, garden flowers. And you're right. They have rounded, almost shield-shaped leaves with stems connected to the middle of the leaf and stunning horn-shaped flowers that bell at the ends in yellow, orange, and red.

But, nasturtium leaves and flowers, are tasty as well as beautiful. Their peppery flavor resembles that of watercress, the elegant salad green. Although it isn't related, watercress curiously bears the genus name of nasturtium.

Grown primarily for their flowers, nasturtiums have been one of the lesser known herbs. About the only reference to them as medicinal plants occurs in the writings of Pliny, who thought they would enliven a sluggish person. The species he was writing about could not have been the nasturtium so commonly seen now, as it is a native of South America, but it may have been a related plant. It is said too that nasturtium juice is good to reduce itching.

Care and Cultivation

Nasturtiums are tender annuals, started by sowing seed outdoors as soon as the ground warms and there's no danger of frost. They do best in a sunny area with well-drained fertile soil. The large, round seeds are covered with about an inch of soil, which should be gently pressed down over them. Germination takes 7 to 12 days. Thin the seedlings to allow space for the plants to develop their characteristic viny

65

growth. They can be allowed to hang down slopes, climb up rocks, run over the compost heap, or just run along the ground. The space each plant needs will depend on where it's allowed to go.

As soon as the leaves appear, harvesting can begin. You may take either leaves, flowers, or flower buds; but plan to use them fresh, when they are most flavorful.

How To Use Nasturtiums

Both nasturtium greens and flowers make delightful additions to salads or sandwiches, much like lettuce, where their slightly pungent and spicy flavor is appreciated. The seeds, too, can be used to make an old Chinese treat; simply pickle them in vinegar and store for later eating enjoyment. Nasturtium flower buds can be used as a substitute for capers and they have a similar taste. The best use for nasturtiums: as a companion plant in the garden. They not only add color, but also protect other plants by repelling a number of insects and collecting (for easy removal) some others—such as aphids.

Parsley

Petroselinum crispum ● Umbelliferae family

Parsley, unfortunately, spends more time brightening meals with its color than as a flavoring. Some say 90 percent of all parsley used is never eaten. While hard to surpass in this regard, it can be one of the most useful culinary herbs as well. This unsung herb is pleasantly flavored, amazingly versatile, and virtually a storehouse of vitamins A, B, C, and E, plus iron and other minerals. Yet many Americans know it only as the green ruffly sprig left on restaurant plates.

The ancient Greeks didn't eat it either, though for different reasons. They valued parsley highly. Enough to crown the victors of their games and feed it to chariot horses, which according to Homer made them run faster. The herb was honored medicinally as a cure for digestive ailments and its use even extended to prevention of intoxication. Parsley garlands were worn to lavish banquets, supposedly absorbing the alcoholic fumes of wine. The herb was also associated with funerary ritual, and sprigs were scattered on tombs and graves.

The Romans, however, did eat parsley, enjoying it as a culinary herb, and appreciating its breath-freshening capability as well as respecting its medicinal virtues.

This esteem was reversed with medieval European superstition. Folk tales told of parsley growing best in the garden of a witch or when planted by a pregnant woman. A similar variation reports that it grew well only in homes dominated by women. Another story, related to parsley's long germination period, reasoned that parsley's seed had to go to the devil seven times before it grew. Ultimately, parsley was the sure harbinger of bad luck, a myth intensified by the herb's habit of dying when transplanted.

Surviving the abuse, the herb firmly established itself in the British Isles by 1548. Parsley then spread from England to the rest of the world, readily adapting to climates quite unlike its native Mediterranean region.

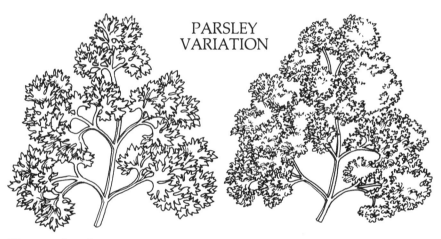

PARSLEY VARIATION

Description

The variety of parsley most commonly grown is French parsley, or species *crispum*. It's noted for leaves that are fluted, curled, serrated, and in every way frilled to create a mass of delicate, intensely green foliage. Moss curled, triple curled, and curled are all names given to this French variety. Parsley typically grows 12 to 20 inches high, spreading out to nearly a foot. Flowers that form in little umbrellas grace the plant in its second year, crowning it with greenish yellow.

There is an Italian variety of parsley, which though more flavorful, is less attractive. It has plain, dark-green leaves with little curl and less serration.

Care and Cultivation

Prior to planting, it's important to soak the seeds in warm water overnight. This will speed germination by as much as several days. With transplanting ruled out, the seeds are sown in the plant's final home—either outdoors or indoors. Sow 1/4 inch deep in moist, rich soil where the plants will receive ample sun, but are protected from high heat on the hottest days of summer. Parsley germinates in 3 to 4 weeks and needs to be well weeded and watered at the start. Thin to 10 inches apart when 2 inches tall, remembering not to crowd.

Though parsley is a hardy biennial, it's generally grown as an annual to ensure a fresh supply of tender, first year leaves. You may harvest the leaves as you are ready to use them, taking the oldest ones first. The leaves may be dried quickly in the shade for later use, though some flavor will be sacrificed.

How To Use Parsley

Second to none as a garnish, parsley adds color to the plate and freshens the breath when chewed at the end of the meal. When added to foods, its gentle quality overcomes excess garlic and onion flavors, blending nicely. Parsley can be added to nearly any dish that isn't sweet, including soups, stews, dressings, salads, and omelettes.

The gardener will enjoy parsley as a lush green border, and other plants can benefit from growing near the herb. Plant it between carrots and onions, or with tomatoes and asparagus.

Rosemary

Rosmarinus officinalis Labiatae family

Legend tells that while fleeing to Egypt, the Virgin Mary spread her lovely azure cloak on a rosemary bush, which responded by turning its flowers the same blue color. Many are surprised, hearing this story, that the common name, rosemary, did not come from this tale. It is derived instead from the Greek scientific name for the plant, *Rosmarinus*, meaning "dew of the sea." The name alludes to the place where rosemary grew wild—near the Mediterranean, often within reach of the salt sea sprays.

The early Greeks believed rosemary was good for the brain, and thus would improve memory. Greek students wore rosemary wreaths at examination time in hopes it would aid their recall. As rosemary spread throughout Europe, so did this notion, and gradually the herb came to be associated with fidelity through fond remembrance. From medieval times on, wedding bouquets contained rosemary, and sprigs were given to lovers. Even funerals saw use of rosemary, and it often was placed on the casket to assure long remembrance by friends and family.

Medieval herbalists believed rosemary could cure nervous problems, even to make one youthful, lively, and lusty. A brew of rosemary, called Hungary water, was recommended for the nerves as late as 1759.

There were also many superstitions in which rosemary was favored to ward off evil, particularly witchcraft and the "evil eye." Likewise, it was assumed to thrive only in the gardens of good people.

Rosemary's fresh fragrance was appreciated in more than bouquets—it was mixed with juniper berries in an incense to purify French hospitals. A practice beginning in medieval times, this use was discontinued only recently.

Description

Rosemary is a bushy, woody shrub, covered thickly with small, pine-needlelike leaves that are dark-green on top and a lighter gray-green beneath. Small blue or white flowers, depending on the variety, grace the ends of the evergreen branches in spring and summer, though some flowers are found year-round on indoor plants. Height ranges from 2 to 6 feet when mature, with the average bush growing between 2 and 3 feet and spreading at least as wide.

Care and Cultivation

Rosemary is grown most readily from 6-inch cuttings, planted 4 inches deep. Plants may be layered by burying some of the lower branches until they develop roots. If you cannot obtain a cutting, try starting from seed. It will take 2 or 3 years to develop a plant that can yield a large harvest, but some say that plants grown from seed are the best.

Sow *thickly* indoors, 1/8 inch deep, in early spring. The soil should be light, well drained, and slightly alkaline. Sheltered sun or shade should be provided in the beginning. Germination takes 2 to 4 weeks, and only a few of the seeds will germinate successfully. Herb growers have experienced as little as 15 percent germination.

When the seedlings are 6 inches tall, transplant to 3 feet apart. If you live in a mild climate, transplant outdoors. In colder regions, keep rosemary as an indoor plant, or be prepared to cover and mulch heavily outside.

Harvest usually can begin the second year, when new growth in the middle of the plant is cut back to encourage bushing. Cut sparingly at first, more as the plant matures. The cut stems are used fresh or can be dried in the shade.

How To Use Rosemary

While rosemary leaves are almost a necessity for poultry and stuffings, they're also used with other meats; they can be rubbed on roasts, beef or pork before cooking. For a special barbecued chicken, use a rosemary sprig to brush on the sauce while cooking, and then put sprigs on the charcoal to smoke during the final roasting. If you make jelly to accompany lamb or veal, use rosemary leaves instead of mint for a pleasing, complementary taste.

A strong rosemary tea can be used as a hair rinse to decrease dandruff and impart a pleasant scent.

As a garden companion, rosemary likes growing with sage and carrots, and will help protect members of the cabbage family from pests.

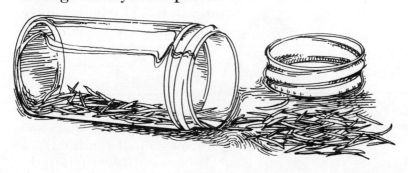

Rue

Ruta graveolens Rutaceae family

*I*f your interest in herbs is just beginning, rue may not be as familiar to you as many of the others. Its history is primarily medicinal, dating back to the early Greeks and later the Romans, who used it to remedy insect bites, ward off disease, as an antidote to poisons, and in herbal preparations used to restore sight. Pliny, herbal chronicler of ancient Rome, mentioned rue as a remedy for as many as 84 different ailments. Even the name of the plant reflects these supposed healing benefits, coming from the Greek *reuo* meaning "to set free."

The pungent, musky smell of rue fared well throughout the Middle Ages and carried with it the belief that the herb would protect people from witches and wild beasts. This was perhaps based on its ability to repel insects, and its use by the church. Rue was regarded as the herb of repentance and the herb of grace by the church. It was often used in sprigs to sprinkle holy water prior to the celebration of High Mass.

Rue found its way to the English criminal court around 1750. For the judges sitting at Assize, the sprigs of rue that dotted the dock benches held at bay the fleas, contagion, and unpleasantness that came with the prisoners brought before the bench.

In more recent times, legend has quieted, and rue has taken on a more civilized, domestic role. It is principally grown today as a decorative hedge and a garden companion. Rue has been used as a culinary herb, but these instances are rare. Most notably the French used it as a minor kitchen herb, and the Italians used it to flavor an herbal vinegar. This is largely due to the herb's strong smell and bitter taste.

It's been found, too, that rue can produce an allergic reaction similar to that of poison ivy. Though not all people are affected, problems may easily arise if any large quantities are ingested.

Description

Rue is an herb of contrasts. Its robust appearance and powerful aroma are offset by its delicate, almost fern-like foliage. Small, oval leaves with slightly blunted ends alternate up the woody stem, which terminates in equally tiny greenish-yellow flowers that open throughout the summer. A mature rue plant will reach nearly three feet in height and bush out to about two feet.

Care and Cultivation

Rue is easily started either indoors (to start it for transplanting) or outdoors. It should be sown indoors in late winter, outdoors in early spring, and covered with 1/8 inch of fine soil. It does well in full sun and heavy, poor soil. The seed germinates easily in 10 to 14 days, and the young plants should be thinned to stand 18 inches apart when they reach 1 to 2 inches tall. If started indoors, rue can be transplanted easily. Harvest before the plant flowers.

How To Use Rue

Rue is used primarily as a very becoming border hedge that flowers continuously throughout the summer months. In the fall, it bears an attractive seed pod, which can be used in dried arrangements. The leaves can be used in herb vinegars, but it is cautioned that it be used sparingly. It is useful, though, to repel flies and as a companion plant for raspberries and roses. Do, however, keep it away from basil, which it seems to dislike.

Legend had it that arrows tipped with the juice of rue would always strike true. Modern archers rarely employ this technique possibly due to the scarcity of the herb.

Sage

Salvia officinalis Labiatae family

*I*n modern times this herb has been used mainly as a culinary accent, with sage dressing accompanying the Thanksgiving turkey, virtually an American tradition. In contrast, the ancients used sage almost entirely as a medicinal herb.

Greeks and Romans of the time of Dioscorides and Pliny thought sage to be a general cure-all, particularly useful to promote longevity. Indeed, the scientific name of sage, *Salvia*, derives from the Latin word meaning "to save" or "to heal." Sage was reputed to be a general tonic for the mind and body, thus contributing to long life. It was even reported to cure snakebites.

Attitudes toward sage as a medicine remained much the same through the time of Culpeper and Gerard, and as late as the 1700's, Sir John Hill agreed that it stimulated the memory and senses, was generally good for the head, and improved palsy.

Sage traveled to China with the Dutch traders, and the Chinese appreciated its medicinal virtues, but used it for something new —tea. Sage tea was so popular that the Chinese would trade three to four pounds of Chinese tea for one pound of sage. Other traditional uses, the origins of which have been forgotten, are as a mouthwash, tooth cleanser, and as a darkener for graying hair.

Description

     The variety of sage most commonly grown, *Salvia officinalis,* or garden sage, varies greatly in appearance. In general, it is a many-branched plant, growing 14 to 20 inches high, with light gray-green leaves that have a rounded, oblong shape and are covered with short silver-gray hairs. The stem is squarish and also covered with hair. Flowers in blue-to-purplish whorls decorate terminal spikes with color in late August.

     Individual plants show different colors, and the typical heavily veined leaves vary considerably in pattern.

Care and Cultivation

     Sage is a hardy perennial that becomes woody after three or four years. It should be resown frequently enough to keep it from getting tough. It is sown thinly, 1/4 inch deep, in loose, calcium-rich soil where it receives full sun. Seeds are started indoors in early spring, outdoors in late spring, and germinate in 10 to 20 days with even moisture. Thin 12 to 18 inches apart. If you start them indoors, you may transplant outside in late spring, but consider sage as a house plant too.

     The first year, sage is harvested lightly no later than September to ensure wintering. In later years, two harvests are possible. Harvest the new growth and dry in the shade.

How To Use Sage

     Sage seasons rich, fatty meats such as pork and fowl, and when used in relatively large quantities helps reduce the gamy flavor of wild duck and goose. Its taste can also be enjoyed in cheeses, sausages, and soufflés.

     Sage grows well with rosemary and protects cabbage and carrots, but should be kept away from cucumber plants. Bees use sage pollen to make one of the finest honeys you'll ever taste.

     A word of warning to those who live in the Western United States: The sagebrush that grows on the high plains and in the mountains is not the same sage, even though it has a somewhat similar smell and bees make good honey from it.

Summer Savory

Satureia hortensis Labiatae family

Summer savory is a sweet-scented, tangy-tasting herb used throughout history to enhance the flavors of a multitude of dishes, ranging from meats and beans to stuffings.

The Romans enjoyed a vinegar made with savory as a sauce to accompany their rich meals, and its use as a peppery seasoning is recorded long before the first black pepper reached Rome from the East.

Virgil, remembered more as a poet than a beekeeper, believed the sweet smell of summer savory would attract bees and improve their honey. Though it is primarily a culinary herb, Culpeper listed a number of medicinal uses for summer savory: as a carminative, a treatment for asthma, and even, he thought, a cure for deafness.

Today, summer savory is not used as a medicine, and its uses are limited to the kitchen. It is so compatible with bean dishes that it has become known as the "bean herb."

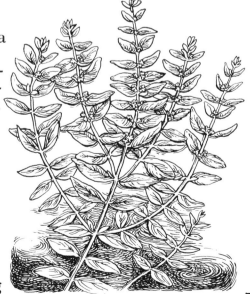

Description

Summer savory is a pleasing complement to the gray herbs in your garden, displaying bladelike, short, deep-green leaves that turn reddish in the fall. It flowers in mid-July, sprouting bunches of light-pink, white, or lavender flowers at the leaf axils. Height is 12 to 18 inches.

Care and Cultivation

Summer savory is a hardy annual that does well indoors and out, growing rapidly throughout its growing

75

season. Start from seed, sown thinly 1/8 inch deep in late spring, in rich, well-drained soil. Seeds germinate in 7 to 14 days when kept moist and given diffused light. Seeds do not germinate well if more than a year old.

Thin to 6 inches apart when the seedlings are 2 inches tall. Plenty of water is needed to keep up with the fast growth. The herb is easily transplanted if you wish it outdoors.

Summer savory leaves are harvested by cutting back the tops of stems throughout the summer and then cutting the whole plant when it decides to flower. The leaves may be frozen or dried—they dry rapidly and easily.

How To Use Summer Savory

An endless list of dishes are enhanced by summer savory. The most common ones are eggs, poultry, meat, stuffings, sauces, green salads, and especially beans. Add summer savory to the cooking waters of turnips, brussel sprouts, cabbage, and other strong-smelling vegetables to reduce unpleasant odors in the kitchen. Tea from savory leaves is pleasing, as is savory-flavored vinegar.

Summer savory accompanies onions and green beans both in the garden and on the table.

Tansy

Tanacetum vulgare Compositae family

The rich fernlike appearance of tansy is perhaps its most endearing quality. It brings to the garden lush green growth, reminiscent of the dense coastal forests of the Pacific Northwest. It's a commanding plant, both in terms of size and appearance, and will beautifully complement the lower-growing plants in your garden. Tansy's feathery leaves are deeply dissected, about 4 inches wide and 6 inches long, with a wavy, serrated edge similar to that of many ferns. The leaves branch out from a single stem that rises 3 to 4 feet in height.

Tansy's beauty in the garden peaks in late summer, when it blooms, producing button-shaped yellow flowers in clusters at the tip of the stem. The tightly packed head on a disc is the characteristic flower shape of the

76

sun-loving *Compositae* family, which includes such relatives as tarragon, the marigold, the dandelion, and sunflower.

History and Uses

Primarily a medieval medicinal herb, tansy was recommended as a cure for gout, plague, and colic. It also was used as a spring tonic to stave off summer ills. People in Sussex even put tansy leaves in their shoes to ward off ague. Because of its potent aroma when bruised and its strong, bitter-tasting leaves, tansy was not widely used as a culinary herb, which may have been well. Some modern authorities assert it may be poisonous if ingested in more than minute quantities. As a flavoring tansy is so strong that one would normally find it unpleasant; yet it was used in medieval teas, puddings, and Lenten cakes, which became known as "tansies." Tansies were eaten on Easter day as a reminder of the bitter herbs eaten by the Jews at Passover. It was written in the 1600's that consuming tansy was beneficial after the salt fish and meager diet of Lent.

Care and Cultivation

Tansy is a hardy perennial, which may be one way of saying "Many Happy Returns." It has been suggested that the plant's name, tansy (being derived from the Greek *athanasia*, meaning immortality), implies more than an ancient use and encompasses the herb's tenacity and abundance. As each season ends, the plant will die back, to grow up again in the spring.

Tansy is less hardy in the beginning, but with a little care and coaxing it can be started from seed. Once established, spreading is rapid because of an aggressive root system. If let go, it may rapidly overrun the garden. The easiest way to deal with this is to skirt the problem, using galvanized grass edging to barricade the roots. Keep the plants widely separated (20 inches suggested) to allow them to spread their beautiful leaves. Sow thinly and cover lightly with fine soil, keeping the soil evenly moist until the seeds germinate in two to three weeks. Leaves may be harvested for teas and tansy cakes, or the entire plant may be harvested for drying after the flowers form.

How To Use Tansy

Tansy at its best is a decorative, hardy border for gardens, and is known to repel flying insects and ants. The leaves may be used sparingly in omelettes and salad dressings. The entire plant is used in decorative flower arrangements, both fresh and dried. Whether you actually harvest tansy or not, you will enjoy it as a beautiful addition to your herb garden.

Tarragon

Artemesia dracunculus / Artemesia redowski Compositae family

Tarragon, an herb essential to French cooking, is a relative newcomer to the world of herbs. Its use as a culinary herb is known to extend back to the late 1500's, but prior to that it appeared in herbal literature only rarely.

The ancients believed it would draw poison from venomous bites and used it in treating the bites of rabid dogs. Hippocrates recorded it as a useful medical herb and referred to it as one of the "simple," or one-herb, remedies. From that point on, little of tarragon was heard, except for a superstition that held it could increase stamina. Trusting this to be true, pilgrims were known to have put it in their shoes as an aid on their long and tiring journeys.

Sometime in the 1500's, Europe discovered what a delight the flavorful tarragon really is. Since then its popularity has consistently increased. The taste, likened to anise and licorice, is required for a proper Sauce Béarnaise, and appears frequently in vinegars, a variety of fish and meat dishes, and in many cold sauces. Medical uses for tarragon have been totally forgotten in deference to its wonderful taste.

The name tarragon is derived from the French *esdragon*, which in turn stems from Latin *Dracunculus*. Both the Latin and French mean "little dragon," from which tarragon takes its popular name of "dragon herb." The reasons behind this name are only hypothetical—with some evidence to support the theory that it is derived from the serpentine appearance of the plant's root.

Description

Tarragon is an erect, shrubby plant with slender long branches rising to a height of about 2 feet. The leaves are thin and bladelike and highly aromatic. French tarragon, species *dracunculus*, has smooth, glossy, dark-green leaves and small, inconspicuous green flowers that open in midsummer. These flowers rarely, if ever, produce seed. The more vigorous Russian variety, species *Redowski*, is coarser, less pungent, and seeds readily. It occasionally grows to a greater height than the French variety.

TARRAGON: THE DRAGON HERB

Care and Cultivation

Primarily a culinary herb harvested for its flavorful leaves, French tarragon is the more desirable of the two tarragons. It can, however, be started only if you can get a cutting or a root division. Purchasing it involves some risk, simply because many gardeners don't differentiate one variety from the other. What you purchase as French may very well be Russian.

The Russian variety that starts easily from seed is still well worth growing. A hardy perennial, its demands are few; it grows well in a medium-rich soil and partial sun. Seeds are sown thinly in early spring and covered with a fine layer of soil. With even moisture, the seeds germinate in 10 to 14 days. Tarragon needs a little room to

79

spread its lateral roots. Thin to stand 18 inches apart and keep well weeded and watered. As plants mature, they should be allowed to dry out thoroughly between waterings.

Harvest the entire plant when the lower leaves turn yellow, and follow the techniques outlined in the drying section of this book. Fresh sprigs may be snipped for cooking at any time.

How To Use Tarragon

Tarragon is wonderful in any cold meat sauces because of its spicy sweetness, and is a welcome addition to eggs, cheese, and fish. It's an essential element in many French dishes. To make tarragon vinegar, fill a bottle with fresh sprigs and add a good white-wine vinegar. Soak at least a few hours before straining.

Thyme

Thymus vulgaris Labiatae family

"*I've often been inclined to grow herbs and finally I have the thyme.*" –Anonymous Regardless of how seriously you take your gardening, the urge to make puns about this herb is difficult to resist, and is probably one of the chief reasons behind its familiarity. "Punning thyme" is a centuries-old sport of English-speaking people.

The ancients looked on thyme with a more serious eye. To the classical Greeks the invigorating qualities of the herb epitomized both bravery and courage, standing as a symbol for honorable action. Indeed, one possible etymology may be the Greek word for courage. It was a high compliment to tell someone he or she smelled of thyme, which may have been literally true, as the plant was used for scent. Allusions to thyme's ability to instill courage persisted into the Middle Ages, when it was customary for a lady to embroider a bee and a sprig of thyme on a scarf and present it to her hero prior to battle.

Though thyme has been enjoyed for its marvelous aroma and pleasing taste, historically it was, and still is, an important medicinal herb. The ancients thought that it cured melancholy as well as imparted strength. In fact, as late as the eighteenth century, thyme was recommended as a cure for hangover by the noted botanist and taxonomist Carl Linneaus. More recently, a distillate of thyme called thymol was used as an antiseptic in World War I and is still an important ingredient in mouthwashes, gargles, and coughdrops. Thymol is reputed to cure hookworm in horses and dogs, to relieve skin irritations, and is the fungicidal agent in preparations that prevent mildew, and cure meat.

Thyme is one of the legendary sweet-smelling herbs that graced the manger of Christ, and even today the smaller varieties are often grown in cracks of walkways, where continual bruising releases the pleasing fragrance.

As a culinary herb, thyme finds its way into nearly any meat, fish, or vegetable dish, and even into many liqueurs, such as Benedictine.

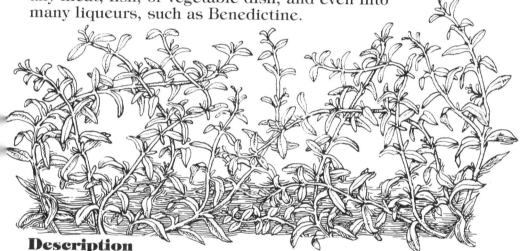

Description

Thymus vulgaris is the most popularly grown of the hundred or so varieties of thyme. A small, bushy, semierect plant, it grows nearly a foot high and is covered with tiny gray-green leaves that are 1/4 inch long or less. These narrow leaves profusely cover a woody stem which sports small lavender flowers from May to August.

Varieties include both erect and creeping plants with similar small leaves, some of which are covered with fine hairs. The more common variations are called creeping thyme, silver thyme, woolly thyme, and lemon-scented thyme.

Care and Cultivation

This herb is a tender perennial, grown easily from seed by sowing in light, dry, well-drained soil that receives full sun. It is started indoors, where an even temperature (around 70°F) and steady moisture will assure a 5 to 10 day germination. When seedlings are 2 to 3 inches tall, they can be transplanted to stand 8 inches apart, and may be moved outdoors when the weather warms. Thyme also makes a good house plant, which may be taken outdoors in its pot for the summer. Keep well weeded.

Harvest by cutting the entire plant to 2 inches above ground before it flowers in early summer. Dry the leaves in the shade. A second growth should be left if the plant is to winter outside.

How To Use Thyme

Clam chowder and other fish soups take much of their distinctive taste from thyme, and it universally seasons soups, stews, sauces, and meat dishes. Its potent flavor indicates moderate usage.

As a companion plant, thyme will repel cabbage moths. Herb gardeners find it most attractive when grown around rocks, its natural habitat. Thyme is noted for its ability to attract bees and other pollinating insects. The honey produced from thyme flowers is superb by connoisseurs' standards.

Yarrow

Achillea millefolium Compositae family

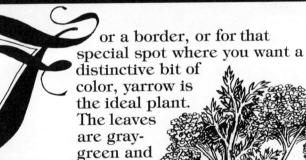

For a border, or for that special spot where you want a distinctive bit of color, yarrow is the ideal plant. The leaves are gray-green and divided so that they resemble downy plumes, giving the herb its species name *millefolium*—"thousand leafed."

When it blossoms, yarrow will dominate the garden with its wide bunches of small flowers in white, yellow, orange, or pink to deep, purplish red.

Its modest height of about 2 feet allows yarrow to take a prominent place in your garden—right up front where you can enjoy its elegance.

History and Uses

In the past, yarrow was appreciated more for its medical benefits than for its beauty. In fact, it received its genus name of *Achillea* from a legend that Achilles used it to heal wounds during the Trojan War.

Historically it's been used as a snuff, as a toothache remedy, and at times as a stand-in for hops in brewing beer. Romantic folklore also implies a kind of cure: Yarrow, when placed under the pillow would bring visionary dreams of future loves.

Today, even though yarrow is grown mainly for its beauty, it still finds a place as a medicinal aid because of its styptic, stringent, tonic, and sweat-inducing properties.

Care and Cultivation

Yarrow is a perennial so hardy that it grows wild in many places and sometimes is considered a weed. Though it prefers light sandy soil and full sun, it will grow under almost any conditions.

Happily for the beginning gardener, yarrow is easily started from seed—indoors in early spring, outside in late spring. The seeds are pressed firmly into the bottom of a one-inch-deep furrow, but not covered. Light ensures good germination, which generally takes 7 to 12 days. Thin or transplant to stand 4 inches apart. Yarrow grows well in clumps and transplants easily.

Harvest by cutting the entire plant while in full bloom, and dry quickly in the shade to retain the flowers' color.

How To Use Yarrow

Grown for its flowers, yarrow is often dried and used in bouquets, which brighten the home for months with color and a sage-sweet smell. The flowers come in a variety of attractive colors, the reds being the most striking.

Yarrow brews into a medicinal tea, often prescribed by many herbal doctors. In the kitchen, yarrow may be used occasionally instead of cinnamon or nutmeg, but this use is limited.

In the herb garden, yarrow makes aromatic plants more potent, while adding its lovely flowers and elegant leaves.

The stalks of yarrow have traditionally been used in casting the *I-Ching*, an ancient Chinese text of divination. Advice on life situations is said to be revealed in the random tossing of coins often substituted by yarrow stalks.

Recipes & Culinary Uses

As we've stated, the United States has changed from a "salt and pepper" nation to one interested in the fine nuances and culinary flare offered by herbs and spices. Within the last decade, our country has experienced at least a 70 percent overall increase in demand for herbs and spices.

One reason for our recent herbal revival may be attributed to an expanded interest in foods of many nationalities. First generation European minorities from Italy and France brought recipes with them from the old country which called for such exotic herbs as marjoram, basil, thyme, fennel, and many others. South Asian immigrants, too, brought with them the exciting spices and herbs native to their cuisine. Indians, for instance, can use up to fifteen different herbs and spices just to make their own personal blend of curry for flavoring lamb, chicken, or vegetables.

Many primitive areas developed recipes incorporating spices and herbs native to their particular regions. When explorers discovered the route to the Spice Islands, these precious buds of flavor were brought to Europe for the tables of the wealthy. Gradually the tastes followed the patterns of migration to the United States.
Now the children, grandchildren, and great-grandchildren of first generation Americans have spread to all corners of our nation, taking with them the culinary taste treats of their native lands.

Chains of Mexican, Italian, and other specialty and ethnic restaurants have sprung up nationwide to disperse their unique cuisines. What makes them unique? Chili would not be chili without cumin seed in one form or another; a pizza would have a flat taste without the familiar sprinkling of oregano; and hamburger buns would be just plain bread if we eliminated those pearls of flavor, sesame seeds.

In addition to home uses for herbs, industrial and institutional uses have become exceedingly important.

Many public relations campaigns promote new food products. The use of secret spices and herbs is often publicized to entice the consumer to try a new taste treat.

We encourage you to experiment with the culinary herbs. Our recipes are basic but can be varied to your taste once you become familiar with the characteristics of the different items on your herb shelf.

Remember: dried herbs should be stored in tightly covered containers away from heat or light, as they tend to lose flavor with exposure to either. And, fresh herbs perform best when just clipped from your own plantings.

BASIL *Ocimum basilicum*

Classic Italian Tomato Sauce

This sauce flavored with basil is the basis for most other fancier Italian sauces. It is very easy and especially good when vine-ripened tomatoes are available.

2 1/2 tbs. olive oil
1/2 cup chopped onions
4 tbs. tomato paste
2 1/2 cups chopped
   Italian plum tomatoes or
   undrained cut canned tomatoes

1 cup water
1 1/2 tbs. fresh basil
   or 4 tbs. dried basil
1/2 tsp. salt
1 tsp. sugar (to cut acidity)
Ground pepper to taste

Heat olive oil in heavy 4-qt. sauce pan. Oil should be very hot. Add onions and cook until soft. Combine remaining ingredients and cook very slowly. Partly cover and cook for 50 minutes, stirring occasionally.

Puree finished sauce in a blender. Adjust seasoning.

CAYENNE PEPPER *Capsicum annum*

Spicy Bar-B-Que Sauce

Cayenne pepper and ground hot peppers can be counted on to give a good, spicy kick to any recipe. Cayenne is often available in liquid form as hot pepper sauce.

2 1/2 cups catsup
1 1/2 tsp. cayenne pepper
1/2 cup corn oil
1 1/2 tbs. brown sugar
1/2 cup lemon juice
1/3 cup distilled vinegar
1 tsp. dry mustard

2 tsp. hot pepper sauce
2 cups onions, freshly chopped
2 cloves garlic, freshly chopped
1 bay leaf
2 whole cloves
1/3 cup water
Salt to taste

Heat oil until slightly smoking. Add onions and cook until clear. Add garlic and cook for one additional minute. Add remaining ingredients and bring to a boil. Reduce immediately to simmer and cook uncovered for 15 to 20 minutes. Sauce may be used on spareribs, chicken, or other meats. To vary flavor, add herbs such as tarragon, chives, parsley, or sage.

CHIVES *Allium schoenoprasum*

Chive and Sour Cream Omelette

Chives, the delicate relative of the common onion, are a great addition to eggs, dips, salads, and sauces. The flavor is far "greener" and lighter than that of onions.

5 fresh large eggs
3 tbs. sweet butter
2 tbs. freshly snipped or dried chives
1/4 cup sour cream
Salt and pepper to taste
Dash of Worcestershire sauce

Beat eggs lightly in bowl; add chives and seasonings. Melt butter in omelette pan until it bubbles, but don't let it get brown. Add eggs and lightly move pan back and forth over a high flame while stirring contents with fork. When eggs congeal to your taste, turn heat off, and spread sour cream over eggs. Tilt pan forward and fold omelette from front of pan onto a warmed platter. Serve at once.
Serves 2.

CORIANDER *Coriandrum sativum*

Coriander Chicken

Coriander, a spice prized in Europe and the East for years, is finally coming to its deserved prominence in the United States. Its flavor is bright and complements bland meats very well.

1 chicken 2 1/2 to 3 1/2 lbs. cut in eighths
4 cloves minced garlic
4 tbs. ground coriander
2 cups coarsely chopped onions

1/2 cup lemon juice
1/2 cup corn oil
1/2 cup soya sauce
3 tbs. sugar
Hot sauce to taste
Ground Fresh Black Pepper

Combine all ingredients in bowl and marinate chicken for 4 to 6 hours. Remove chicken from marinade, pat dry, and broil or barbecue. Cook marinade in sauce pan by bringing to a boil and reducing to simmer for 35 to 45 minutes. After chicken is cooked, serve cooked marinade on chicken.
Serves 3 to 4.

DILL *Anethum graveolens*

Dilled Chicken Soup

Dill herb and dill seed are wonderful flavoring ingredients. They are from the same plant at different stages of development. Dill is great in soups, salads, rice, and condiments.

1 quartered chicken 4 to 5 lbs.
2 quartered large onions
2 well cleaned leeks
4 carrots cut in 5 pieces
2 parsnips scraped and cut
1 tbs. salt

1/2 tsp. black Pepper
1 bunch dill herb
  (handful of leaf stalks)
1 bunch parsley
  (about 5 stalks)
Water to cover all ingredients

Place all ingredients in heavy 6-8 quart pot. Add water to cover ingredients. Bring soup to boil; skim top of pot. Reduce heat to simmer and partially cover. Cook for 2 1/2 to 3 hours. Strain ingredients from soup. Remove excess fat and serve soup with chicken and vegetables. Leftover soup can be frozen for use in dozens of other recipes.

Serves 6 to 8.

SWEET MARJORAM *Marjorana hortensis*

Tuna Salad with Marjoram and Capers

Marjoram is closely related botanically to oregano. The sweet variety is more delicate than the wild type and is wonderful for pepping up tuna.

1 9 1/2-oz. can tuna fish in oil
1 tbs. lemon juice
1 tsp. Worcestershire sauce
3 tbs. mayonnaise

1/2 tsp. dried marjoram
1 tbs. capers in vinegar
1/2 tsp. salt
Freshly ground pepper

Press oil out of tuna. Place tuna in bowl and flake into small pieces. Add remaining ingredients and mix well. Serve on bed of lettuce or as a sandwich spread.

OREGANO *Origanum vulgare*

French Tomato Salad

Oregano is one of the distinctive flavor ingredients in many Southern European food preparations. It is familiar in pizza as well as an important ingredient in Mexican dishes.

4 ripe tomatoes, sliced thick
2/3 cup olive oil
1/4 cup wine vinegar
2 tbs. lemon juice
2 cloves garlic, crushed

2 tbs. chopped parsley
1/4 cup water
1/2 tsp. dried oregano
1/2 tsp. basil (dried)
1/2 tsp. salt
Ground black pepper

Combine all ingredients and marinate for at least 2 hours. Chill well before serving. Excellent as a first course or side salad.

Serves 4.

PARSLEY *Petroselinum crispum hortense*

Parsley unfortunately spends more time as a garnish than in actual cooking. Some say 90 percent of the parsley purchased is never eaten. The following is an excellent recipe, which heavily depends on parsley for flavor. Green sauce is used as a dressing, cold or hot, for all types of vegetables. It uses other green herbs for flavor as well.

Parsley Green Sauce

1 cup olive oil
1/4 cup wine vinegar
2 tbs. lemon juice
2 tbs. finely chopped dill
2 tbs. capers (drained)
2 tbs. finely chopped onions

1 clove minced garlic
1/2 cup finely chopped parsley
1 small boiled potato
 (finely chopped)
Salt and pepper, freshly
 ground, to taste

Combine vinegar and lemon juice in mixing bowl. Slowly add oil, beating ingredients with a wire whisk. After contents are somewhat creamy, fold in other ingredients. Add salt and pepper to taste. Makes 2 1/2 cups. Sauce can be used on cold or warm cooked string beans, broccoli, cauliflower, and other vegetables.

ROSEMARY *Rosmarinus officinalis*

Rosemary, a mint relative, is native to Spain and North Africa. It is a hearty and fragrant herb that goes well with lamb, chicken and shrimp, as well as many vegetables such as turnips, green beans, tomato salad and squash. Since rosemary is strong in flavor it should be used with a light hand.

Lamb Chops Español

4 shoulder lamb chops 3/4" cut
2 tbs. olive oil
2 tbs. sweet butter
1 large sweet onion, chopped
1 green pepper, chopped

1 small can tomatoes
3/4 tsp. dried rosemary
 (or 2 tsp. fresh)
Salt and pepper to taste
Flour

Combine 1/2 cup flour, salt and pepper in plastic bag. Lightly flour the lamb chops and set them aside. Heat 2 tbs. of olive oil in large skillet. Brown lamb chops over medium-high heat, cooking for 3 to 4 minutes on each side. After browning, reserve on heated platter in warm oven.

In same skillet, drain excess fat and heat 2 tbs. sweet butter and cook onions for 4 minutes. Add green pepper, cooking both together for 8 to 10 minutes, or until pepper begins to soften. Add drained tomatoes. Cook one more minute until mixture is warm. Add crumbled rosemary leaves. Put sauce over warmed lamb chops. Adjust seasoning.

Serve immediately on warmed platter surrounded with rice.

Serves 2.

SAGE *Salvia officinalis*

This dried silver-gray herb is related to mint. It is prized as a sausage seasoning in our country. The herb is grown primarily in Yugoslavia and Albania and is incorporated in food in its leaf form rubbed or powdered. In our sausage recipe, we use rubbed sage.

Family Style Sausage
2 lbs. lean pork (Boston Butt)
3/4 lbs. salt pork, ground
1 tbs. coarse salt
1 tsp. chopped shallots (or garlic)
1 large onion, chopped fine
1 tsp. rubbed sage

1 tsp. ground mace
2 tsp. fresh cracked pepper
2 tsp. ground parsley
1/2 tsp. Allspice, ground
1/2 tsp. Cloves, ground

Combine all ingredients thoroughly. Fry in hot skillet until crispy and well cooked, or stuff in sausage casing and fry or broil thoroughly.

Makes about 3 pounds.

SAVORY *Satureja hortensis*

Savory, another relative of the mint family, is a wonderful, tasty herb used extensively in bean dishes. It is also an interesting flavoring for cheese, as described below.

Savory Cheese Spread
8 oz. softened block cream cheese
8 oz. softened blue cheese
1 tsp. Worcestershire sauce
1/4 tsp. hot chili sauce
Ground black pepper
1 tbs. dried savory leaves

Combine softened cheeses, add Worcestershire sauce, chili sauce, and pepper. Mix well and roll into a ball. Refrigerate for at least an hour and just before serving, sprinkle savory on the cheese ball, and press in lightly so that it appears on the surface of the cheese. Serve with crackers or thin slices of fresh French bread.

TARRAGON *Artemisia dracunculus*

Although it has an aniselike aroma, tarragon is related to the aster. It is a prized herb used in vinegars and salads, and it is indispensible as a contribution to the following poultry recipe.

Chicken Tarragon

4 chicken breasts, skinned, boned, and pounded thin
2 eggs
6 tbs. clarified sweet butter
4 tbs. finely minced shallots
Salt
Freshly ground white pepper
1 tsp. crumbled dried tarragon
3/4 cup heavy cream
Flour for dredging

Dredge breasts in beaten egg and then in flour seasoned with salt and pepper. Sauté breasts in clarified butter for 4 minutes on each side. Begin with 3 tbs. of butter and add as needed. Remove lightly browned breasts from pan and reserve on heated serving dish. Sauté shallots in pan drippings. Add wine, deglaze pan drippings and reduce wine by half. Add tarragon and heavy cream, after pan is removed from heat. Pour sauce over chicken breasts and serve immediately.
Serves 4.

THYME *Thymus vulgaris*

Thyme could be called the herb of Provençal, France. Its unmistakable flavor is used in the family-style one-pot meals of Southern France. It has been adopted as the main herb flavor of much-loved New England and Manhattan Clam Chowder.

Quick Manhattan Clam Chowder

2 large onions, finely chopped
1 clove garlic, minced
1/4 lb. smoked bacon
   in one chunk
1 large can minced clams
1 bottle clam juice
1 can whole, cooked tomatoes,
   drained and minced

6 boiled and diced
   new potatoes
1 tsp. dried thyme leaves
2 bay leaves
1/2 tsp. salt
1/2 tsp. freshly ground pepper
1 cup water

Render bacon in heavy 3-4-qt. pot. Sauté onions and garlic until clear but not brown. Add clams, clam juice, tomatoes, potatoes, and water. Bring to a boil. Reduce heat to simmer. Add seasonings and continue to simmer for 20 minutes. Serve hot with oyster crackers.
Serves 2 to 3.

Vinegars

Herbal vinegars, once the tools of gourmet chefs in fine restaurants, can now be made and enjoyed by anyone with a garden. The most popular vinegar, tarragon, is by no means the only option. Virtually every herb that you grow and use for cooking can be the main ingredient in a herbal vinegar.

A good imagination and a little experience with seasonings can enable you to create a "house" vinegar that will make your greens stand up and take a bow.

Herbal vinegars are by no means limited to the following selection, but here is a start:

Anise	Coriander	Parsley
Basil	Dill	Peppermint
Borage	Fennel	Spearmint
Caraway	Garlic	Savory
Catnip	Lemon Balm	Tarragon
Cayenne	Marjoram	Thyme
Chives	Oregano	

General Directions

Start with a good quality red or white wine or a cider vinegar. Wash enough sprigs of your chosen herb to fill a glass jar. Add enough vinegar to cover the herb and cap tightly. Store in a warm sunny location for two to three weeks. Shake daily. At the end of this period give your vinegar the taste test. If you feel it's not strong enough, strain it off and add more fresh leaves, using the same process as before. When satisfied with the final result, strain and bottle with one or two sprigs of the fresh herb for decoration.

91

Almost any combination of herb will work with vinegar. If you're a beginner—just imagine that you are making an oil-and-vinegar salad dressing. The herbs might be basil, marjoram, garlic, and a touch of thyme. A host of pleasing combinations can be developed with experience.

Herbs with delicate flavors such as tarragon or borage dictate a lighter white wine vinegar, while the heartier taste of the stronger herbs will come through the more robust flavor of a cider or red wine vinegar.

Extra Bonus

If you can make herbal vinegars you can also make herbal oils using the same technique. Bland oils are best to use as a base, since they have little scent of their own to mask the infused herbs. Safflower or corn oil works well. Wash the herbs and allow to air-dry before adding the oil. Place the covered glass jar in strong sunlight. Shake the oil every few days to make sure that the maximum amount of the herb gets infused. The herbal oil may take a while longer to make, since a vegetable oil will not extract as well as a vinegar. Steep your blend for three to four weeks before testing the oil. It should have the distinctive odor of the herb when a little is rubbed on the skin. If your oil is not strong enough, add some fresh herb cuttings and steep again as you did the vinegar. Your herbal oils can be used to flavor salad dressings, sauté meats or vegetables, or as cosmetic oils for your skin.

Libations

Alcohol can be another convenient vehicle for consuming your abundant supply of fresh herbs. For some the opposite is also true! Whichever the case, both wine and grain alcohol make excellent extracting mediums. Once again follow the vinegar technique. The one exception is the sunlight. You don't need it. In fact, a dark cupboard would be best. Shake the brew daily and strain in ten days.

The sweet and the minty herbs readily lend themselves to extracting in brandy or other cordials. A little ice cream with a flavored liqueur topping makes an excellent dessert.

Turning Over a New Leaf

The potential uses of herbs are by no means exhausted once you have crumbled the leaves of your homegrown plants over a cooking pot. Although cooking traditionally has been an important way to use herbs, they also have many other facets. Teas, shampoos, herbal baths, hair dyes, salves, medicines, and ointments are just a few of the ways we use herbs daily.

The following pages describe several interesting and practical methods to use the herbs that you may grow. The inspired enthusiast, however, will find a wealth of directions and recipes beyond the few given here. Suggested readings are listed at the end of this book, and we heartily invite you to explore them.

Teas are simple to prepare and a joy to drink. Either fresh or dried herbs can be used to make them, simply by varying the amount of herb. For dried herbs, the general recipe is: Pour one cup of boiling water over one teaspoon of herb. Steep three to five minutes, strain, and serve. When using fresh herbs, ordinarily you can use four times the dried amount. Finely chop the fresh leaves, add the boiling water, and steep as usual. Iced herb teas, a summertime favorite, are made by doubling the amount of the herb. Steep normally, then refrigerate or add ice. The reason for the stronger brew is: The cold desensitizes your taste buds, therefore, the tea must be more potent in flavor to taste the same to you. A sprig of fresh herb is often added to cold teas as a colorful garnish.

The following herbs are commonly used alone or in combination when making herb teas:

Catnip	Horehound	Lemon Balm	Sage
Chamomile	Hyssop	Peppermint	Spearmint
Comfrey	Lavender	Rosemary	Yarrow

Here's a recipe you'll like—authentic Moroccan Spearmint Tea that's served in homes, cafés, and restaurants throughout the "land farthest west" from Rabat to Fez, Oujda to Essaouira.

1 tall glass	Sprigs of fresh spearmint
3 tablespoons sugar	to fill the glass
or honey	Boiling water

Put sugar or honey and spearmint in the glass. Pour the boiling water over the leaves. Steep in thoughts of Tangier nights while your tea brews. Drink with the spearmint still in the glass.

Cosmetics originally were composed entirely from materials which were plant or animal in origin. Only the recent past has brought about a change, which popularized ingredients of synthetic origin. However, as the public has become aware of the detrimental effects inherent in some of these synthetics, there has been a return to the natural, the less complex. Certainly sensitivities to plants or their essential oils are not unknown, but these are hardly reactions to ingredients that cause skin cancer or make your hair fall out.

The commonly used cosmetic herbs are:

Angelica	Chamomile	Lemon Balm	Sage
Basil	Comfrey	Parsley	Spearmint
Catnip	Fennel	Peppermint	Thyme
Calendula	Lavender	Rosemary	Yarrow

By combining 1/3 cup each of rosemary leaves, chamomile flowers, and raspberry leaves, you can make a scalp and hair conditioning rinse that will add fragrant highlights to your hair. All three ingredients are available at health food stores if you aren't growing them.

Begin by pouring one quart of boiling water over the herbs and allow to steep for twenty minutes. Strain the mixture, and pour over freshly shampooed hair, catching the tea in a basin. Repeat five to ten times, making sure that all your hair has been covered. Dry your hair as you would normally.

The same conditioner will also work well as a facial. Heat the tea until it just begins to steam. Remove it from the heat, with the herbs still in it, and put it directly under your face. Place a towel over your head, forming a small tent that will keep the steam in. Breathe deeply and let the herbs open your pores and cleanse your skin while you enjoy the aroma. Continue as described for five to ten minutes.

To make a spearmint facial, combine in a blender the fresh spearmint leaves and one of the following oils: wheat germ, sesame, avocado, almond, coconut, or safflower. Start with about 1/2 cup of oil and add enough spearmint leaves to make a solution the consistency of thin hand lotion. Apply the lotion to a clean face and relax for a few minutes. Wash it off, using a mild soap if necessary, and pat dry. This is a great treatment for those hot summer nights.

Herbal soap can be made an easy way, starting with a cup of strong tea from one or more of the following herbs: calendula, chamomile, comfrey, fennel, lavender, lemon balm, parsley, peppermint, sage, spearmint, thyme, or yarrow. Put the mixture in a sturdy glass jar, and add a bar of unscented or lightly scented soap that has been grated through a carrot grater. Place the jar in a pot of boiling water and cook the mixture for about twenty minutes. Pour it into a cardboard mold shaped like a cake of soap. Cover with a towel and let it cool slowly. The soap will be completely set up in a day or two, after which all you do is enjoy.

Traditional Applications

The haze of antiquity obscures the day when early man first used herbs for healing. Modern man has had access only to the folk wisdom and writings of herbalists for the past two or three millenia; a relatively recent period when viewed against their ancient beginnings. Though early herb uses often appear absurd, or steeped in superstition, modern science has borne out many of the time-tested recipes created by our forefathers. Research has shown that horehound does have expectorant properties, just as any old-time druggist would have told you when selling you horehound cough drops. Comfrey, called "knit bone" in the old days, has been found to contain allantoin, a substance now recognized for its healing capabilities.

Traditional uses of herbs as medicines, then, are of interest to modern medicine and to the herb gardener who wishes a complete historical perspective on the plants in his garden. It is cautioned, though, that the uses given here to fulfill the gardener's historical interest are not ones that should be employed for treatment of ailments. Old-time remedies have developed through folklore and folk wisdom, both of which often quarrel with modern science.

Angelica Angelica leaf or root tea has been employed as a remedy for coughs and colds. It was considered to be a stimulating expectorant and a good bronchial and stomachic tonic. A fresh poultice of the leaves was also said to help draw out poisons and aid healing.

Anise The fruit of the anise plant is a major ingredient in the potent liqueur anisette, considered a bronchial tonic. For the less adventuresome, a tea was made from the seeds for a soothing cough remedy.

Basil First-aid for insect stings and bites was thought to be near at hand if basil grew in the garden. A fresh poultice of two or three leaves was used to ease the bite.

Borage When put into wine, it was said that the leaves and flowers of the borage plant would make men and women glad,

95

merry, and drive away all sadness, dullness, and melancholy. Inflamed swelling or bad bruises were also treated with borage in an externally applied poultice of mashed fresh leaves.

Catnip Catnip's minty taste and mild diaphoretic action helped to bring sleep and freer perspiration to fever patients, yet was considered to be mellow enough to be used with children for upset stomachs.

Cayenne Herbalists considered this one of nature's most potent natural stimulants. Cayenne given to chickens in the winter kept them active, warm, and laying eggs regardless of the cold. In days past, when feet never seemed to warm up after October, a daily dose till spring was the time-honored recipe. Cayenne was also used for a sluggish circulation.

Chamomile The fragrant tea of chamomile flowers soothed jangled nerves and calmed an upset stomach. When Peter Rabbit ate too many greens his mother wisely gave him chamomile tea. A strong tea also makes an herbal hair rinse that is used by blondes.

Comfrey Both the leaves and roots contain allantoin, a substance recognized for its healing properties. Taken internally, comfrey made not only a great all-round tonic, but had even been used in earlier times to arrest internal hemorrhaging. A healing poultice of fresh mashed leaves was used to soothe and heal burns, rashes, sprains, and cuts. It has also been used to ease the pain of rheumatism and arthritis.

Dill & Fennel These two plants from the Unbelliferae (umbrella) family were thought to have much the same medicinal action. A mother's friend, an infusion of the seeds helped to increase the quantity and quality of mother's milk, and helped to relieve flatulence when given to her young one.

Garlic The "Super Bulb" once had a reputation of preventing the plague, a reputation undoubtedly started before the plague swept through Europe. There are stories, however, of scavenging bands that roamed through plague-swept villages looting from the dead. Their immunity from sickness was attributed to the garlic they wore and ate in excess. More recently garlic has come under scientific scrutiny. Researchers are exploring claims of its powers as a natural antibiotic.

Horehound Whatever became of horehound drops? A great old-fashioned cough remedy, people used to make their own by boiling fresh leaves, adding raw sugar and cream of tartar.

Hyssop A poultice of fresh, crushed leaves was the standard method of soothing bruises, and was used especially to treat a black eye. This poultice was also used in relieving the pain of rheumatism.

Lemon Balm Supposedly a cooling tea for fever patients, this merry brew, drunk daily, was also thought to be beneficial in promoting a long life and an active mind.

Oregano Herbal history suggests a warm poultice of oregano was used to soothe sprains, bruises, and swellings.

Parsley One of nature's finest diuretics, fresh parsley and parsley root tea were taken liberally for mild complaints or obstructions of the kidneys. Fresh parsley is also loaded with vitamins. Be sure to include it in salads, and don't leave this garnish on your plate.

Mint Many of the mints, especially peppermint and spearmint are very soothing and settling to the stomach. Both of these are also mildly stimulating. A cup of mint tea in the morning is a pleasant substitute for coffee. An old home remedy for the flu was made by brewing together equal parts of peppermint and elder flowers and drinking freely until the fever subsided.

Rue The "herb-of-grace" has been used since antiquity to ward off contagious diseases. It has also been used as a tonic tea to stimulate circulation, and the juice expressed from rue was used to clear up an earache. However, allergic reactions were not uncommon.

Sage In Old England this member of the mint family was often rubbed directly on the teeth and gums to whiten the teeth and strengthen the gums. Good tasting sage tea was thought to be a tonic for the stomach, a blood cleanser, and is said to have helped suppress mammary secretions during weaning.

Tansy From the cradle to the grave, the ancients found uses for tansy. It was used both to increase fertility in women and as an abortive. Throughout life, tansy was applied to calm hysteria, remove freckles and soothe sprains. In the end, the fern-like tansy leaf was an indispensable ingredient for embalmers.

Thyme Famous for the honey it yields, thyme is also one of nature's most powerful antiseptics. Its oil (thymol) is useful as a germicide and disinfectant, and is commonly found in dentifrices and mouthwashes.

Yarrow Achilles on the battlefield is said to have used the fresh yarrow leaves to heal the wounds of his injured soldiers. Yarrow was also used to treat fevers and colds by drinking a hot tea made from the leaves.

An Herbal Library

*From the very beginning The Helix Herbal Album was
designed to stimulate an interest in herbs and make it easy for you to begin a
garden. As your garden becomes green and full, and your interest blossoms,
you'll want or need information that's not available in our book.
For this reason we've included the following collection of books for
further reference.*

A Modern Herbal. M. Grieve. 1971.
Dover Publications, Inc. New York.
      Maude Grieve is one of the most distinguished
herbalists of our time. This is her technical reference book for the
herbal gardener. Each of the plant descriptions, which number in
the hundreds, contain a botanical description, chemical
constituents, medicinal action and use. An excellent reference
book for those seriously interested in herbs.

The Book of Spices. Frederic Rosengarten, Jr. 1973.
Pyramid Books. New York.
      This book is written more as a layman's introduction to
the spice trade than an herbal, but it does well in both areas. You
will not find much information on growing, but it does contain
some interesting reading on the commercial uses of herbs and
spices, production, and history. It contains a complete section of
recipes for each herb.

The Complete Book of Fruits and Vegetables. Francesco
Bianchini and Francesco Corbetta. 1975. Crown. New York.
      This is an Italian book written in English with large,

very well-drawn illustrations of hundreds of plants. A brief description of each plant is included. The same authors have another book, *Health Plants of the World*. Francesco Bianchini and Francesco Corbetta. 1977. Newsweek. New York., which is also excellent.

Culinary Herbs and Condiments. Maude Grieve. 1971. Dover Publications, Inc. New York.

A more in-depth study of culinary herbs than her book, *A Modern Herbal*. An excellent book for traditional uses and recipes.

Encyclopedia of Herbs. Renny Harrop, ed. 1977. Chartwell Books Inc. New Jersey.

The most beautifully designed and executed book on herbs that we have found. This is a British book that is sold only in the United States. It may be difficult to locate, but well worth the effort. The beautiful color pictures and illustrations are a delight even to those with little herbal interest. Over forty brief descriptions in the herbal section are adorned with large color plates that look like ancient woodcuts. The recipe section stands out like no other. The photographs alone are enough to satiate a starving man. We highly recommend it and give this book an A+.

Handbook of Plant and Floral Ornament. Richard G. Hatton. 1960. Dover Publications, Inc. New York.

A complete guide to plant forms and shapes, classified by family names. Artwork is selected from the herbals of the sixteenth century. The finest examples of plant-drawing found in those rare works.

The Herbal Body Book. Jeanne Rose. 1976. Grosset and Dunlap. New York.

If it's at all possible to use an herb on some part of your body, this book will probably tell you how. Very interesting reading filled with recipes ranging from the common to the absolutely absurd.

Herbs. James Underwood Crockett and Ogden Tanner. 1977. Time-Life Books. Virginia.

Full-color photographs and illustrations make this an enjoyable, easy-to-read book. There are many excellent pictures of herb gardens and individual herbs with over a hundred herbs listed in the encyclopedia section, many with color illustrations. It contains some useful climatic and herbal-characteristic charts at the end of the book.

Herbs. Magda Ironside Wood, ed. 1976. Marshall Cavendish. New York.

This is a beautifully comprehensive, color-packed book of growing, drying and using herbs—from cooking to cosmetics.

How to Grow Herbs. Richard Osborne, *et al.* the editors of Sunset Books and Sunset Magazine. 1974. Lane Magazine and Book Company. California.

   This book is filled with black-and-white photographs and has brief sections on all aspects of herbs with a few recipes and short descriptions of about forty herbs. A good beginning book.

Llewellyn's Moon Sign Book and Daily Planetary Guide. Llewellyn. 1977. Llewellyn Publications. Saint Paul, Minnesota.

   Besides an abundance of astrological information, the *Moon Sign Book* has devoted a whole section to the farm and garden. This section contains information on companion planting, lunar planting, and the best harvesting times. It also details traditional herbal remedies in a special section, conveniently categorized by ailment.

The Oxford Book of Food Plants. S.G. Harrison, *et al.* 1975. Oxford University Press. London, England.

   Full-color drawings of almost all plants that are consumed as food. Annotated with brief descriptions of each plant and interesting facts.

The Rodale Herb Book. William H. Hylton, ed. 1976. Rodale Press, Inc. Emmaus, Pennsylvania.

   This book contains more information on herbs than any other. Complete information on: using herbs as medicine, herbs for cooking, other uses for herbs, growing, propagation, harvest, and storage of herbs, companion herbs for pest control, landscaping, and herb gardens. This is the standard reference book for herb gardening, written with the down-home style common to the Rodale publications.

	ANNUAL	PERENNIAL	BIENNIAL	HEIGHT	SPREAD	FULL SUN / PARTIAL SUN	SEEDS	CUTTINGS	ROOT DIVISION	SOW IN GARDEN	START INDOORS	SOW WHEN MOON IS
						⊙⊖	PROPAGATION					
Anise	Tender			2'	6"	⊙	easy			✓		● new
Basil	T			20"	12"	⊙	easy			✓	✓	○ full
Borage	Hardy			16"	20"	⊙	easy			✓		○
Calendula	H			18"	12"	⊙	easy			✓		○
Caraway			H	30"	6"	⊙	easy			✓		○
Catnip		H		30"	12"	⊙	slow	✓			✓	○
Cayenne	T			30"	18"	⊙	easy				✓	○
Chamomile		H		24"	18"	⊙	easy			✓	✓	○
Chervil	H					⊖	easy			✓	✓	○
Chives		H		16"	6"	⊙	easy		✓		✓	○
Comfrey		H		30"	24"	⊙	easy		✓		✓	○
Coriander	T			30"	6"	⊙	easy			✓		○
Dill	H			3'	6"	⊙	easy			✓		○
Fennel			H	3'	18"	⊙	easy		✓	✓	✓	○
Garlic	H			18"	6"	⊙	no	✓	✓			●
Horehound		H		14"	20"	⊙	slow	✓			✓	○
Hyssop		H		3'	2'	⊙	easy	✓			✓	○
Lavender		T		20"	24"	⊙	slow	✓			✓	●
Lemon Balm		T		30"	S	⊙	slow	✓	✓		✓	●
Marjoram	H			10"	S	⊙	easy			✓	✓	○
Nasturtium	T			18"	12"	⊙	easy			✓		●
Opal Basil	T			20"	12"	⊙	easy			✓	✓	○
Oregano		T		12"	S	⊙	easy	✓		✓	✓	○
Parsley			H	18"	12"	⊙	slow			✓	✓	●
Peppermint		H		20"	S	⊖	slow		✓		✓	●
Rosemary		T		30"	36"	⊙	slow	✓			✓	●
Rue		H		3'	2'	⊙	easy	✓			✓	○
Sage		H		18"	18"	⊙	easy			✓	✓	○
Spearmint		H		20"	S	⊖	slow		✓		✓	●
Savory	H			16"	8"	⊙	easy			✓	✓	○
Tansy		H		3'	3'	⊙	slow		✓		✓	○
Tarragon		H		20"	18"	⊙	easy		✓		✓	○
Thyme		T		12"	10"	⊙	easy	✓	✓	✓	✓	●
Yarrow		H		24"	12"	⊙	slow		✓		✓	○

	USES				PARTS			HARVEST					WINTER		
	TEA	SEASONING	MEDICINAL	COSMETIC	LEAVES	SEEDS or FRUIT	FLOWERS/TOPS	AS NEEDED	BEFORE FLOWERING	WHILE IN FLOWER	WHEN SEEDS TURN	DRY RAPIDLY	CUT BACK	LEAVE FOLIAGE	MULCH IN NORTH
Anise		•	•			•						•	•		
Basil		•			•			•	•			•	•		
Borage	•				•		•	•	•	•			•		
Calendula				•			•			•			•		
Caraway		•	•			•					•			•	
Catnip	•		•		•			•	•	•			•		•
Cayenne		•	•			•		*					•		
Chamomile	•		•	•			•			•			•		
Chervil		•			•			•	•				•		
Chives		•			•			•	•				•		
Comfrey	•		•	•	•				•				•		
Coriander		•	•		•	•		•			•		•		
Dill	•	•	•		•	•		•			•		•		
Fennel	•	•	•		•	•		•			•		•		
Garlic		•	•			•		*					•		
Horehound	•		•		•				•					•	•
Hyssop	•		•		•				•					•	•
Lavender				•	•		•		•	•				•	•
Lemon Balm	•				•			•	•					•	•
Marjoram		•			•				•				•		
Nasturtium		•			•			•	•	•			•		
Opal Basil		•			•				•				•		
Oregano		•			•				•				•		•
Parsley	•	•	•		•			•					•		
Peppermint	•	•	•	•	•				•	•			•		
Rosemary	•	•			•				•	•				•	•
Rue					•				•					•	•
Sage	•	•	•		•				•					•	•
Spearmint	•	•	•	•	•				•	•			•		
Savory		•			•				•				•		
Tansy		•	•		•		•				•		•		
Tarragon		•			•				•					•	•
Thyme		•	•		•				•					•	•
Yarrow	•		•		•				•	•			•	•	

* See text for specific instructions

Order Form:

Many of the herbs mentioned in this book grow well from seed both indoors and outdoors. Each can be used to add their own unique charm and beauty to your home.

Please record the number of seed packets you want by each herb.

_____ Anise	1000 mg 65ᶜ		_____ Marjoram*	200 mg 49ᶜ
_____ Basil*	500 mg 49ᶜ		_____ Nasturtiums*	1000 mg 65ᶜ
_____ Borage*	1000 mg 49ᶜ		_____ Opal Basil*	500 mg 65ᶜ
_____ Caraway	500 mg 65ᶜ		_____ Oregano*	200 mg 65ᶜ
_____ Catnip*	200 mg 49ᶜ		_____ Parsley*	500 mg 49ᶜ
_____ Cayenne	1000 mg 65ᶜ		(Triple Curl)	
_____ Chamomile*	100 mg 65ᶜ		_____ Peppermint* **	50 mg 49ᶜ
_____ Chervil	300 mg 65ᶜ		_____ Rosemary* **	200 mg 65ᶜ
_____ Chives*	300 mg 49ᶜ		_____ Rue	150 mg 65ᶜ
_____ Coriander	1000 mg 65ᶜ		_____ Sage*	800 mg 49ᶜ
_____ Dill	1000 mg 49ᶜ		_____ Spearmint* **	50 mg 65ᶜ
_____ Fennel	450 mg 65ᶜ		_____ Summer Savory*	100 mg 49ᶜ
(Florence)			_____ Tansy	50 mg 65ᶜ
_____ Horehound	150 mg 65ᶜ		_____ Tarragon*	50 mg 65ᶜ
_____ Hyssop*	200 mg 65ᶜ		(Russian)	
_____ Lavender* **	300 mg 65ᶜ		_____ Thyme*	100 mg 49ᶜ
_____ Lemon Balm* **	200 mg 65ᶜ		_____ Yarrow*	200 mg 65ᶜ
			(Red Flower)	

*   INDOOR/OUTDOOR VARIETY
** This plant is slow to start and is difficult for beginning gardners.

Name _____

Address _____

City_____ State_____ Zip_____

SEND CHECK OR MONEY ORDER TO:

R.F.M. PUBLISHING CORPORATION
P.O. BOX 1299
LONG ISLAND CITY, N.Y. 11101

Please allow three weeks for processing and delivery

WE WARRANT that all Helix Herb Seeds have been tested for germination both in the lab and under actual growing conditions. Each packet of seed is dated, your guarantee that the freshest seed has been used.